INDIVIDUAL CHOICE BEHAVIOR

INDIVIDUAL

GREENWOOD PRESS, PUBLISHERS
WESTPORT, CONNECTICUT

CHOICE BEHAVIOR

A Theoretical Analysis

R. DUNCAN LUCE

PROFESSOR OF PSYCHOLOGY

UNIVERSITY OF PENNSYLVANIA

Library of Congress Cataloging in Publication Data

Luce, Robert Duncan.
    Individual choice behavior.

    Reprint of the ed. published by Wiley, New York.
    Bibliography: p.
    Includes index.
    1. Psychometrics. 2. Choice (Psychology)
I. Title.
[BF39.L8 1979]   153.8'3   78-25881
ISBN 0-313-20778-X

Published in 1959 by John Wiley & Sons, Inc.

Reprinted with the permission of John Wiley & Sons, Inc.,
Publishers.

Reprinted in 1979 by Greenwood Press, Inc.
51 Riverside Avenue, Westport, CT 06880

Printed in the United States of America

10 9 8 7 6 5 4 3 2 1

To my father and mother

PREFACE

Aside from statistics, the most extensive and systematic mathematical applications in psychology have so far centered about problems of organisms making choices from discrete, well-defined sets of alternatives. One need only recall that this is a feature common to information theory, much of psychophysical scaling, utility theory and decision theory generally, stochastic learning theory, and many of the psychometric models. Whether it is a deep or superficial feature is another matter, but there can be little doubt that it exists. If it is deep, one can anticipate considerable benefit accruing to its exposure and study; if not, the study should make clearer some of the inherent differences that have led to a variety of theories. The purpose of this book is to undertake such a study.

A simple probabilistic theory is presented that overlaps each of these fields in a significant way. It by no means subsumes them, but it does seem to be central in part of the development of each. To this common theory each special topic adds conditions of its own that result in its distinctive quality.

The book is theoretical in the sense that it offers a mathematical theory of choice behavior, and it is not empirical in the sense that no new data are presented. It is not, however, anti-empirical. Throughout, questions of empirical verification are considered, and, wherever possible, existing data have been brought to bear. Whether the theory will ultimately have serious empirical consequences remains to be seen, but at the least it has initiated a number of experimental studies which will be reported in the periodical literature.

The material is organized into four main chapters, a summary and conclusions chapter, and four appendixes. The first chapter presents the general theory; it is a prerequisite for the remainder of the book. The next three chapters are devoted to applications of the theory to substantive problems: psychophysics, utility, and learning. Each of these chapters may be read independently of the other two (except that section 4.F depends upon Chapter 3). This means that the book may be used for technical reading in a course on psychophysics without the students having to read the utility or learning chapters or, equally well, in a course on learning without their having to enter into the other topics.

The work described was begun early in 1957 when I was a member of the Departments of Sociology and Mathematical Statistics and on the staff of the Bureau of Applied Social Research, Columbia University, and it was continued after I joined the Department of Social Relations, Harvard University, later that year. Throughout this time it was partially supported by grants from the National Science Foundation (NSF-G2803 and G-4506). During the first stages it was also supported in part by an Office of Naval Research contract for basic research with the Department of Mathematical Statistics, Columbia University.

Many of the results were privately distributed in two mimeographed papers which elicited a number of critical comments that have been of great benefit to me in preparing the final manuscript. In particular, I should like to thank Professors Ernest Adams, John Chipman, Clyde Coombs, Jacob Marschak, Samuel Messick, G. A. Miller, Frederick Mosteller, S. S. Stevens, and Patrick Suppes. In addition, I profited from discussions with a number of the participants in the Social Science Research Council Summer Institute on Mathematical Training in the Social Sciences held at Stanford University in 1957. The next to final draft of the manuscript was read by Mrs. Elizabeth Shipley, Dr. W. S. Torgerson, and Professors R. R. Bush, E. H. Galanter, F. W. Irwin, George Mandler, G. A. Miller, Frank Restle, and S. S. Stevens, each of whom made substantial suggestions toward increasing its clarity and accuracy.

Beyond any doubt, however, my greatest debt is to Professors Bush and Galanter with whom I have discussed intensively these and related matters: their ideas, interest, encouragement, and criticisms have been invaluable. Our discussions were greatly facilitated by a grant from the American Philosophical Society which allowed us to meet periodically.

R. DUNCAN LUCE

Cambridge, Mass.
April 1959

CONTENTS

chapter 1

THE BASIC THEORY

A. INTRODUCTION

One large portion of psychology—including at least the topics of sensation, motivation, simple selective learning, and reaction time—has a common theme: choice. To be sure, in the study of sensation the choices are among stimuli, in learning they are among responses, and in motivation, among alternatives having different preference evaluations; and some psychologists hold that these distinctions, at least the one between stimulus and response, are basic to an understanding of behavior. This book attempts a partial mathematical description of individual choice behavior in which the distinction is not made except in the language used in different interpretations of the theory. Thus the more neutral word "alternative" is used to include the several cases.

In essence, the approach taken—in this respect, by no means novel—is orthogonal to that of *S-R* psychology, but not at variance with it. Rather than search for lawfulness between stimuli and responses and attempt to formulate a theory to describe those relationships, we shall be concerned with possible lawfulness found among different, but related, choice situations, whether these are choices among stimuli or among responses. Possibly the simplest prototype of this type of theory is the frequently assumed rule of transitivity among choices: given that a person chooses *a* over *b* and that he chooses *b* over *c*, then he chooses *a* over *c* when *a* and *c* are offered. This assumption, were it true, would be a law relating a person's choice in one situation to those in two others, not a law relating responses to stimuli.   It is evident that a sufficiently rich set of relations of this sort, coupled with a few simple *S-R* connections, will allow one to derive many more, and possibly quite complicated, *S-R* connections.

Such an approach seems to merit careful consideration, since several decades of pure *S-R* psychology have not resulted in notably simple laws of behavior.   However, there seems little point in trying to discuss in detail its merits and demerits now, except to mention it in order to avoid confusion later.   The results that follow—which seem to afford some insight into, and some integration of, psychological and psychophysical scaling, utility theory, and learning theory—will implicitly serve as the argument for the course taken.

1. Probabilistic vs. Algebraic Theories

A basic presupposition of this book is that choice behavior is best described as a probabilistic, not an algebraic, phenomenon.   That is to say, at any instant when a person reaches a decision between, say, a and b we will assume that there is a probability $P(a, b)$ that the choice will be a rather than b.   These probabilities will generally be different from 0 and 1, although these extreme (and important) cases will not be excluded. The alternative is to suppose that the probabilities are always 0 and 1 and that the observed choices tell us which it is; in this case the algebraic theory of relations seems to be the most appropriate mathematical tool.

The decision between these two approaches does not seem to be empirical in nature.   Various sorts of data—intransitivities of choices and inconsistencies when the same choices are offered several times—suggest the probabilitistic model, but they are far from conclusive.   Both of these phenomena can be explained within an algebraic framework provided that the choice pattern is allowed to change over time, either because of learning or because of other changes in the internal state of the organism. The presently unanswerable question is which approach will, in the long run, give a more parsimonious and complete explanation of the total range of phenomena.

The probabilistic philosophy is by now a commonplace in much of psychology, but it is a comparatively new and unproven point of view in utility theory.   To be sure, economists when pressed will admit that the psychologist's assumption is probably the more accurate, but they have argued that the resulting simplicity warrants an algebraic idealization. Ironically, some of the following results suggest that, on the contrary, the idealization may actually have made the utility problem artificially difficult.

2. Multiple Alternative Choices

Once choice behavior is assumed to be probabilistic, a problem arises which does not exist in the algebraic models.   Complete data concerning the choices that a person makes from each possible pair of alternatives taken from a set of three or more alternatives do not appear to determine what choice he will make when the whole set is presented.   Because they cannot escape multiple alternative choice problems economists have been particularly sensitive to this feature of probabilistic models, and it has undoubtedly been one source of their resistance in admitting imperfect discrimination.   Early psychologists, particularly learning theorists, studied multiple alternatives experimentally, but since the data seemed dreadfully complicated a trend set in toward fewer and fewer alternatives until now many studies employ only two.   For the most part, present-day psychologists have been willing to ignore—or, to be more accurate, to bypass and postpone—the connections between pairwise choices and more general ones.   And so the relations have remained obscure.

We shall center our attention on this problem.   The method of attack is to introduce a single axiom relating the various probabilities of choices from different finite sets of alternatives.   It is a simple and, I feel, intuitively compelling axiom that appears to illuminate many of the more traditional problems, in particular the question of whether or not a comparatively unique numerical scale exists which reflects choice behavior. Such a scale, unique except for its unit, is shown to exist very generally. It appears to be the formal counterpart of the intuitive idea of utility (or value) in economics, of incentive value in motivation, of subjective sensation in psychophysics, and of response strength in learning theory.

3. Well-Defined Sets of Alternatives

So far, there seems to have been an implicit assumption that no difficulty is encountered in deciding among what it is that an organism makes its choices.   Actually, in practice, it is extremely difficult to know, and much experimental technique is devoted to arranging matters so that the organism and the experimenter are (thought to be) in agreement about what the alternatives are.   All of our procedures for data collection and analysis require the experimenter to make explicit decisions about whether a certain action did or did not occur, and all of our choice theories—including this one—begin with the assumption that we have a mathematically well-defined set, the elements of which can be identified with the choice alternatives.   How these sets come to be defined for organisms, how they may or may not change with experience, how to detect such changes, etc., are questions that have received but little illumination so far. There are limited experimental results on these topics, but nothing like a coherent theory. Indeed, the whole problem still seems to be floundering at a conceptual level, with us hardly able to talk about it much less to know what experiments to perform.

More than any other single thing, in my opinion, this Achilles' heel has limited the applicability of current theories of choice: it certainly has been a significant stumbling block in the use of information theory in psychology, it has limited learning theory applications to a rather special class of phenomena typified by T-maze experiments, etc. The present theory is no different in this respect from the others.

B. PROBABILITY AXIOMS

Throughout the book we shall suppose that a universal set U is given which is to be interpreted as the universe of possible alternatives (stimuli or responses). In practice U will have to possess a certain homogeneity: the decision maker will have to be able to evaluate the elements of U according to some comparative dimension and to be able to select from certain finite subsets of U the elements that he thinks are superior (or inferior or distinguished in some way) along that dimension. For example, in economics U may be taken to be a set of commodity bundles among which a person can express preferences; in psychophysics it may be the set of possible sound energies (at a fixed frequency) which a subject can be asked to evaluate according to loudness; or in learning theory U may be the set of alternative responses available to the organism. Note that U may be finite or infinite.

In general, a subject is not asked to make a choice from the whole of U but rather from some (small) finite subsets. In a great many experiments only two alternatives are presented to the subject at a time, and he is required to choose the one he prefers or the one he deems louder, etc. Of course, larger subsets could be used, although for the most part they have not been, and certainly most daily decisions are from larger subsets (e.g., the choice of a meal from a menu or the choice among several jobs, etc.).

Let T be a finite subset[1] of U and suppose that an element must be chosen from T. If x is an element of T (written $x \in T$), let $P_T(x)$ denote the probability that the selected element is x. Slightly more generally, if S is a subset of T (written $S \subset T$), let $P_T(S)$ denote the probability that the selected element lies in the subset S. These probabilities are the basic ingredients of the following theory.

---

[1] The restriction to finite subsets is not basic, but for most purposes it does not restrict the applicability of the theory (see, however, Appendix 2), and it introduces considerable simplicity.

In most choice models we would write $P(x)$ for $P_T(x)$ because the choice set T is held invariant throughout the discussion; in fact, we would let T and U be the same set.   Here, however, several different choice sets are to be considered at once.   Let us suppose that we are working with 1000 cps tones at different intensities measured in db above some reference level; let w, x, y, and z denote, respectively, the 50, 52, 54, and 56 db tones. Let $T = \{w, x, y\}$ and $T' = \{x, y, z\}$ and consider choices according to loudness.   There is assumed to be some probability, denoted by $P_T(x)$, that x, the 52-db tone, will be called loudest when T is presented, and another, generally different, probability $P_{T'}(x)$ that x will be called loudest when T' is presented.   There is no reason to expect these probabilities to be the same, and the purpose of the subscripts is to make the several probabilities identifiable.

It must not be forgotten, however, that all of the probabilities having the same subscript T form an ordinary probability measure on the subsets of T.   This means, explicitly, that the following is assumed:

The ordinary probability axioms.

(i) *For* $S \subset T$, $0 \leqq P_T(S) \leqq 1$.
(ii) $P_T(T) = 1$.
(iii) *If* $R, S \subset T$ *and* $R \cap S = \phi$, *then* $P_T(R \cup S) = P_T(R) + P_T(S)$.

Repeated application of part iii implies that

$$P_T(S) = \sum_{x \in S} P_T(x);$$

therefore, it is always sufficient to state results just for $P_T(x)$.

Note that, given our interpretation of these probabilities, part ii means that the subject is forced to make a choice: the probability is 1 that his choice is in T when he must confine his choice to T.

For simplicity of notation, and to conform to standard usage, $P(x, y)$ is written to stand for $P_{\{x,y\}}(x)$ when $x \neq y$.   It will be convenient to introduce the symbol $P(x, x) = \frac{1}{2}$ so that certain equations (e.g., $P(x, y) + P(y, x) = 1$) can be written without any restriction on the values assumed by x and y.

C. CHOICE AXIOM

1. Statement of Axiom

The axioms of ordinary probability theory establish certain restraints upon each of the measures P_T, but no connections are assumed among the several measures.   However, one suspects that, at least for choice behavior, the several measures cannot be completely independent. The relationship we shall investigate can be stated as follows:

Axiom 1. *Let T be a finite subset of U such that, for every $S \subset T$, P_S is defined.*

(i) *If $P(x, y) \neq 0, 1$ for all $x, y \in T$, then for $R \subset S \subset T$*
$$P_T(R) = P_S(R)P_T(S);$$

(ii) *If $P(x, y) = 0$ for some $x, y \in T$, then for every $S \subset T$*
$$P_T(S) = P_{T-\{x\}}(S - \{x\}).$$

Throughout the book the expression "axiom 1 holds for the set T" is used to mean not only that it holds for T itself but also that it holds for every subset of T.

2. Discussion

There are a number of points, both technical and conceptual, that should be made about the axiom.

a. Interpretation. Part ii of the axiom simply states that if y is invariably chosen over x then x may be deleted from T when considering choices from T. This seems reasonable. If one never selects liver in preference to roast beef, then in choosing among liver, roast beef, and chicken one can immediately reduce the problem to consideration of roast beef and chicken.

Lemma 1. *If axiom 1 holds for T and if $P(x, y) = 0$ for some $y \in T$, then $P_T(x) = 0$.*

PROOF. For $z \in T$, $z \neq x$, part ii of axiom 1 implies

$$P_T(z) = P_{T-\{x\}}(z).$$

By parts ii and iii of the probability axioms,

$$1 = P_T(x) + \sum_{z \in T - \{x\}} P_T(z)$$

$$= P_T(x) + \sum_{z \in T - \{x\}} P_{T-\{x\}}(z)$$

$$. = P_T(x) + 1,$$

and the result follows.

By repeated applications of part ii of axiom 1, the choice set can be reduced to one in which only cases of imperfect discrimination ($P(x, y) \neq 0$ or 1) occur, and then part i becomes applicable. So let us consider that part.

To deal with complicated decisions, it is usual to subdivide them into two or more stages: the alternatives are grossly categorized in some fashion and a first decision is made among these categories; the one chosen is further categorized and a second decision is made, etc.   It is commonly accepted, and it is probably true, that when such a multistage process is needed the over-all result depends significantly upon which intermediate partitionings are employed.   One senses, however, that if the decision situation is quite simple—so that a two-stage process is not really needed— then the intermediate categorization, if used, will not matter.   That is to say, the product $P_S(R)P_T(S)$ will not depend upon S.   But, by taking $S = T$, we see that this product must be $P_T(R)$, which is part i of axiom 1.

These remarks make it clear that we cannot expect the axiom to be valid except for simple decisions, but this is no real limitation, since, as we shall see, our results really require only that it be correct for sets of three alternatives.   The question of the range of validity of the axiom is raised again in section 5.B.

The axiom may be viewed in another way provided conditional probability is defined in the usual manner, i.e., if $P_T(S) > 0$, then

$$P_T(R|S) = \frac{P_T(R \cap S)}{P_T(S)}.$$

Lemma 2.   *If $P(x, y) \neq 0, 1$ for all $x, y \in T$, then axiom 1 is equivalent to* $P_S(R) = P_T(R|S)$, *for $R \subset S \subset T$.*

PROOF.   The result is obvious except for the condition $P_T(S) > 0$.   It is clearly sufficient to show $P_T(x) > 0$ for all $x \in T$.   Suppose this were not true for some x, then for any $y \in T$, $y \neq x$, axiom 1.i (p. 6) implies

$$
\begin{aligned}
0 &= P_T(x) \\
&= P(x, y)[P_T(x) + P_T(y)] \\
&= P(x, y)P_T(y).
\end{aligned}
$$

Since $P(x, y) > 0$, it follows that $P_T(y) = 0$, and so $\sum_{y \in T} P_T(y) = 0$, which is impossible by the probability axioms.

Ignoring cases of perfect discrimination, this lemma says that the axiom requires that the measure P_S be identical to the conditional measure induced by P_T.   As a concrete example, suppose that T is the set of entrees on a certain menu, S is some proper subset of T that includes roast beef, and R the single element set of roast beef.   The heart of the axiom is the assumption that when, for whatever reason, the restaurant has only the entrees S the probability of selecting roast beef is the same as the conditional probability of selecting it from S when the whole menu is available.

When first examining part i of the axiom, some have felt that it is tautological; however, the foregoing example should make it clear that a substantive assumption is involved. This can be checked formally by writing out the sample space involved—it will not be done here—or, less formally, by just observing that two distinct experiments are required to verify the axiom. In one T is offered to the subject and P_T is estimated; in the other S is offered and P_S is estimated.

It has been implicit in the discussion, and is explicit in the title of the book, that this theory—axiom 1 in particular—applies to single organisms, not to averages over groups of them. It is not difficult to see that every organism in a group could satisfy the axiom, yet the average probabilities violate it, and vice versa. For example, consider two organisms, 1 and 2, with probabilities

$$P_T^{(1)}(R) = 0.72 \qquad P_S^{(1)}(R) = 0.80 \qquad P_T^{(1)}(S) = 0.90$$

$$P_T^{(2)}(R) = 0.02 \qquad P_S^{(2)}(R) = 0.20 \qquad P_T^{(2)}(S) = 0.10,$$

which satisfy axiom 1 individually. The group averages are 0.37, 0.50, and 0.50, which fail to satisfy the axiom, since $(0.50)(0.50) = 0.25 \neq 0.37$. This does not mean that group studies can never be used in connection with this theory, but they must be chosen with care so as not to do violence to the basic ideas.

b. An alternative axiom. As originally formulated in an unpublished manuscript, the second part of axiom 1 was not given; it was assumed that part i held without restriction. Several examples which are discussed in section 1.D.2 indicate that this is not reasonable. A simple calculation now will suffice to illustrate the difficulty. Suppose that part i held without restriction, that $P(x, y) = 0$, and that $P(x, z) > 0$. Let $T = \{x, y, z\}$. We would then have

$$P_T(x) = P(x, y)P_T(\{x, y\})$$

$$= 0,$$

and

$$P_T(x) = P(x, z)P_T(\{x, z\})$$

$$= P(x, z)[P_T(x) + P_T(z)].$$

Since $P_T(x) = 0$ and $P(x, z) > 0$, it follows that $P_T(z) = 0$. That is to say, unrestricted application of part i means that if y is always preferred to x and if, however infrequently, x is sometimes preferred to z then z is never chosen from the set of the three. Intuitively, this does not seem correct.

c. **Independence from irrelevant alternatives.**

Lemma 3.   *If $P(x, y) \neq 0, 1$ for all $x, y \in T$, then axiom 1 implies that for any $S \subset T$ such that $x, y \in S$,*

$$\frac{P(x, y)}{P(y, x)} = \frac{P_S(x)}{P_S(y)}.$$

PROOF.   By the axiom, we know

$$P_S(x) = P(x, y)[P_S(x) + P_S(y)],$$

so

$$P_S(x)[1 - P(x, y)] = P_S(x)P(y, x) = P(x, y)P_S(y).$$

From the proof of lemma 2 we know that none of the probabilities is 0, so cross-dividing gives the result.

The essential fact contained in lemma 3 is that when axiom 1 holds for T and its subsets the ratio $P_S(x)/P_S(y)$ is independent of S.

In decision theory (see, for example, Luce and Raiffa [1957]) one axiomatic idea, which may be termed "independence from irrelevant alternatives," is recurrent.   The idea was brought to the fore by Arrow [1951] in a particular choice context, but the same basic notion appears in other contexts in which, of course, its axiomatic formulation differs somewhat.   Arrow termed his axiomatization of the idea "independence of irrelevant alternatives," but, as Professor S. S. Stevens has pointed out to me, this phrase is unfortunately misleading, since it suggests that the irrelevant alternatives are independent of one another.   The actual gist of the idea is that alternatives which *should be* irrelevant to the choice are in fact irrelevant, hence the present term.   For example, the idea states that if one is comparing two alternatives according to some algebraic criterion, say preference, this comparison should be unaffected by the addition of new alternatives or the subtraction of old ones (different from the two under consideration).   Exactly what should be taken to be the probabilistic analogue of this idea is not perfectly clear, but one reasonable possibility is the requirement that the ratio of the probability of choosing one alternative to the probability of choosing the other should not depend upon the total set of alternatives available, i.e., the assertion of lemma 3. In this sense, then, we can say that axiom 1 is *a* probabilistic version of the independence-from-irrelevant-alternatives idea.

It should be noted that it is only the ratio of the two probabilities, not the probabilities themselves, that is invariant with changes of the irrelevant alternatives; thus axiom 1 is not clearly at variance with *Gestalt* ideas, as it might first seem.

d. **Transitivity.**   In choice work in which discrimination is assumed to be perfect it has been customary to assume that pairwise choices are transitive. It would be unfortunate if axiom 1 were at variance with this assumption; it is not.

Lemma 4. *If axiom* 1 *holds for* $T = \{x, y, z\}$ *and if* $P(x, y) = 1$ *and* $P(y, z) = 1$, *then* $P(x, z) = 1$.

PROOF. Since both $P(y, x) = 0$ and $P(z, y) = 0$, part ii of axiom 1 implies that $P_T(x) = P(x, z) = P(x, y)$, but, by assumption, $P(x, y) = 1$, hence the assertion.

Thus axiom 1 is a probabilistic version of two of the more important axioms in nonprobabilistic choice theory: independence from irrelevant alternatives and transitivity.

e. Alternative formulations of part i. Other ways of stating part i of axiom 1 are possible, but, as they seem to shed but little light on its meaning and they are not needed in the sequel, they have been relegated to Appendix 1.

3. Previous Work

So far as is known, no one has proposed and investigated an axiom exactly equivalent to axiom 1; however, in several places part i of the axiom has arisen.

a. Conditional probability theory. After the main ideas reported here were developed, Professor Patrick Suppes called to my attention papers by Császár [1955] and Rényi [1955] that are closely related to this work. Their problem was to axiomatize conditional probability. Without going into any of the niceties of probability theory, let me sketch their main idea. Suppose, first, that a probability measure p is given on a suitable class of subsets of a set U, then for the subsets S and T such that $p(T) > 0$ the conditional probability of S given T is defined as

$$p(S|T) = \frac{p(S \cap T)}{p(T)}.$$

Now, if $R \subset S \subset T$, then

$$p(R|S)p(S|T) = \frac{p(R \cap S)}{p(S)} \frac{p(S \cap T)}{p(T)}$$

$$= \frac{p(R)}{p(S)} \frac{p(S)}{p(T)}$$

$$= \frac{p(R \cap T)}{p(T)}$$

$$= p(R|T).$$

This is, of course, the formal analogue of part i of axiom 1.   By taking three arbitrary sets, instead of $R \subset S \subset T$, a somewhat more general condition can be shown to hold.   They take this more general property as an axiom for conditional probability when no unconditional probability measure is given.   In the traditionally general manner of abstract probability theory they establish the existence of a measure function such that their given probabilities are conditional measures relative to it.   Because of certain empirically reasonable restrictions, a much simpler proof of this same result can be given (see theorem 3 below).   The interpretation and use made of this theorem is considerably different from Rényi and Császár's work.

b. Axiomatic characterization of entropy in information theory. Shannon [1949], in his theory of information, has dealt with certain average properties of choices that are made from a finite set T of alternatives subject to a probability distribution P_T.   A statistic of central importance in his theory—he called it the entropy of the distribution and others have called it the average amount of information transmitted—is

$$H = - \sum_{x \in T} P_T(x) \log_2 P_T(x).$$

Two a priori arguments for using this statistic have been given.   One of these, due to Shannon [1949] and Fano [1949], considers recodings of the messages emanating from the source into "economical" strings of binary digits and shows that in the limit H binary digits are needed on the average for each selection from the source.   This justification may be appropriate when information theory is applied to questions of language and coding, but it does not seem particularly relevant to most of the other uses of information theory in psychology.

The second justification, also due to Shannon, is axiomatic in nature, and it seems to have a reasonable interpretation in many nonlinguistic contexts (e.g., when measuring the amount of information that a subject can transmit about a display of lights).   The most important of Shannon's axioms is the third one in which he assumes that the entropy of a distribution P_T, where T is finite, can always be expressed as the sum of two quantities:

(i) The (unknown) entropy of the distribution that results from the given distribution on T by treating an arbitrary subset S of T as a single element occurring with probability

$$P_T(S) = \sum_{x \in S} P_T(x),$$

plus

(ii) $P_T(S)$ times the (unknown) entropy of the distribution $P_T(x)/P_T(S)$ over the set S.

In other words, Shannon assumes that entropy can be decomposed in a nicely additive manner, using as the distribution over a subset S of T the one naturally induced by P_T. However, if we choose to apply information theory to behavior, as has been done, we must acknowledge that this induced distribution is not necessarily the one actually governing behavior when S rather than T is presented. Therefore, we are only really justified in applying that theory to problems of behavior if we are willing either to accept the recoding justification of the statistic H or to assume that

$$P_S(x) = \frac{P_T(x)}{P_T(S)},$$

which, of course, is part i of axiom 1.

This means that whenever the entropy statistic is used to describe animal or human behavior for which the recoding argument is inapplicable either Shannon's axiomatic defense of the statistic is implicitly rejected or axiom 1 is implicitly assumed. If the latter is true, then information theory implicitly presupposes the consequences of axiom 1, which are relatively strong—specifically, when discrimination is imperfect, it means that choice behavior can be scaled by a ratio scale. Many have believed that information theory could be applied with little regard to the laws satisfied by the organism making the choices, but this seems to be an error.

c. **Constant-ratio rule for confusion matrices.** Clarke [1957] reports studies in which subjects listened to sounds (monosyllables, digits, etc.) drawn from known finite sets of possible sounds but heavily masked by noise. If the noise level is appropriate, a considerable number of errors of identification occur which can be summarized by a square matrix $[P_{ij}]$ of the probabilities of confusion. P_{ij} is the probability that the subject reports sound j when i is actually transmitted. Clarke raises the question: if we know this matrix for a given set T, can we predict the one that will arise when a subset S of T is studied? He proposes using part i of axiom 1, which he has called the "constant-ratio rule" because of the property described in lemma 3. Although he does not explore the implications of his assumption, he does present the only direct empirical test of axiom 1 that has so far been published. His results are discussed presently.

4. Direct Empirical Testing of Axiom 1

a. **The statistical problem.** A discussion of the conditions under which axiom 1 may be expected to hold and something of the role that it might play in the study of choice behavior will not be taken up until a number of its consequences are known (see section 5.B). Since, however, it is clear that, at least in principle, choice data can be collected in specific situations to determine whether the axiom should be rejected there, it is worth considering a few of the statistical issues.

There are various forms in which part i of axiom 1 might be tested, but lemma 3 appears to lead to the simplest results. As shown in theorem 4, the axiom need only be assumed to hold for sets of three elements, so the hypothesis to be tested is that

$$\frac{P(x, y)}{P(y, x)} = \frac{P_{\{x,y,z\}}(x)}{P_{\{x,y,z\}}(y)}.$$

The problem is to get some idea of the number of observations that are needed to have anything like a sensitive test of this hypothesis. An (approximate) expression must be derived for the variance of estimates of these ratios. We know, of course, that if n independent Bernoulli trials are used to estimate each of the basic probabilities p for a single subject, then their variance is $\sigma_p^2 = pq/n$.

Suppose that $f(X, Y)$ is a function that can be expanded in a power series about the two variables X and Y, where X and Y are statistics having means μ_X and μ_Y and standard deviations σ_X and σ_Y, respectively. Of course, we will take $f(X, Y) = X/Y$. Using a linear approximation to f, we have

$$f(X, Y) \approx f(\mu_X, \mu_Y) + (X - \mu_X)f_X(\mu_X, \mu_Y) + (Y - \mu_Y)f_Y(\mu_X, \mu_Y),$$

where $f_X = \dfrac{\partial f}{\partial X}$ and $f_Y = \dfrac{\partial f}{\partial Y}$. Thus,

$$\mu_f = E[f(X, Y)] \approx f(\mu_X, \mu_Y)$$

and

$$\sigma_f^2 = E\{[f(X, Y) - \mu_f]^2\}$$
$$\approx \sigma_X^2 f_X(\mu_X, \mu_Y)^2 + \sigma_Y^2 f_Y(\mu_X, \mu_Y)^2 + 2\rho_{XY}\sigma_X\sigma_Y f_X(\mu_X, \mu_Y)f_Y(\mu_X, \mu_Y),$$

where ρ_{XY} is the correlation between X and Y. A rigorous discussion of this result can be found in Cramér [1946], p. 353.

For our case, $f(X, Y) = X/Y$, so

$$f_X = 1/Y, \quad f_Y = -X/Y^2, \quad \text{and} \quad \rho_{XY} = -\mu_X\mu_Y/n\sigma_X\sigma_Y.$$

Substituting, we find

$$\mu_f = \mu_X/\mu_Y$$
$$\sigma_f^2 = (\mu_X/\mu_Y)^2[2 + (1 - \mu_X)/\mu_X + (1 - \mu_Y)/\mu_Y]/n.$$

If, as in the left side of the equation that we want to test, $\mu_X = 1 - \mu_Y$, then σ_f^2 reduces to $\mu_X/n[1 - \mu_X]^3$.

To gain an idea of the sample sizes needed for the two-alternative case, consider the demand that the standard deviation be some fixed proportion k of the expected ratio, i.e.,

$$\sigma_f = k\mu_X/(1 - \mu_X),$$

then

$$n = 1/k^2\mu_X(1 - \mu_X).$$

The sample sizes for several values of k and μ_X are presented in Table 1; it is clear that rather large sample sizes are required from each subset to obtain reasonably sensitive direct tests of axiom 1.

TABLE 1. **Sample Size n as a Function of μ_X for k = 0.10 and 0.05.** See Text for Explanation of Symbols

k \\ μ_X	0.1	0.2	0.3	0.4	0.5
0.10	1110	625	475	417	400
0.05	4450	2500	1900	1670	1600

b. Clarke's data. As mentioned earlier, the only published data which directly test axiom 1 are Clarke's [1957]. He used the average results from several subjects to estimate the probabilities. As he points out, this is appropriate only to the extent that the subject's probabilities have the same values (see section 1.C.2). Although separate estimates for each subject suggested that their probabilities were similar in this experiment, averaging undoubtedly increased the variance of his results. From data on confusion matrices of one size he predicted the results for smaller confusion matrices. His sample sizes (over subjects and repetitions) ranged from 400 to 1100 per stimulus in different situations. No statistical analysis of the data was presented, but his four scatter diagrams of predicted vs. observed results exhibit a nice linear relation, with apparently no systematic deviations from the 45-degree line. For example, in his first experiment he employed three master sets of six consonants followed by a vowel plus two subsets of three consonants from each master set. Each consonant-vowel pair in a master list was presented 150 times to a subject, and each pair from a three-element subset was presented 200 times. Four subjects and one talker were used. Using axiom 1 (constant-ratio rule), predicted values for the subsets were made from the data on the master sets. The scatter diagram is shown in Figure 1. The results from the other three experiments are similar, with possibly less variance. So, as a first approximation at least, axiom 1 seems to hold in an articulation context.

c. **Time- and space-order errors.**   To test axiom 1 directly, the most reasonable studies appear to be psychophysical.   Not only is it feasible to get the sample sizes needed, but the experimental techniques and controls are better worked out there than in other areas.   There is only one problem: stimuli must be displayed successively either in time or in space, and on many continua there are corresponding time- or space-order errors. For example, let x and y be auditory stimuli that are to be judged according to loudness.   If one presents x and then y and asks which is louder, the probability that x will be chosen is generally smaller than when the order

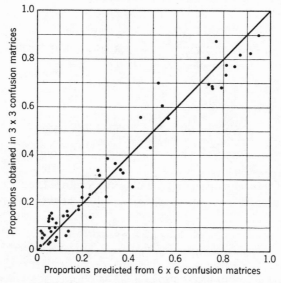

Figure 1.   Scatter diagram of observed proportions of choices in 3 x 3 confusion matrices vs. the predicted proportions obtained by axiom 1 (constant-ratio rule) from the observed proportions in a 6 x 6 confusion matrix.   (Adapted, with permission, from Figure 1, p. 718, Clarke [1957].)

of presentation is reversed.   Space errors are similar but more complex. Neither phenomenon is well understood, and no techniques are known for eliminating them.   Since axiom 1 is stated in terms of unordered sets, it is not immediately clear how one can possibly test it when ordering matters.   This is not an idle problem, since the effects are large when compared with the deviations we should like to detect if axiom 1 is false, and it appears to suggest that we have omitted a basic phenomenon from our theory.   Fortunately, this appearance is misleading, and we are able to encompass these effects in the present theory.   The analysis must be postponed to section 1.F.

D. TWO CONSEQUENCES

1. Statement

The first theorem to be proved establishes formally that if axiom 1 holds all the probabilities are determined by the pairwise probabilities. It is clear that by repeated applications of part ii of axiom 1 we lose no generality in confining our attention to cases in which no discriminations are perfect.

Theorem 1. *If axiom* 1 *holds for* T *and if* $P(x, y) \neq 0, 1$ *for all* $x, y \in T$, *then*

$$P_T(x) = \frac{1}{\displaystyle\sum_{y \in T} \frac{P(y, x)}{P(x, y)}} = \frac{1}{1 + \displaystyle\sum_{y \in T - \{x\}} \frac{P(y, x)}{P(x, y)}}.$$

PROOF.   By lemma 3,

$$\sum_{y \in T} \frac{P(y, x)}{P(x, y)} = 1 + \sum_{y \in T - \{x\}} \frac{P(y, x)}{P(x, y)}$$

$$= \frac{P_T(x)}{P_T(x)} + \sum_{y \in T - \{x\}} \frac{P_T(y)}{P_T(x)}$$

$$= \frac{1}{P_T(x)} \sum_{y \in T} P_T(y).$$

But, by parts ii and iii of the probability axioms,

$$\sum_{y \in T} P_T(y) = 1,$$

hence the assertion.

The next theorem shows that axiom 1 also demands that certain constraints be met by the pairwise probabilities.

Theorem 2. *If axiom* 1 *holds for* $\{x, y, z\}$ *and if none of the pairwise discriminations is perfect, then*

$$P(x, y)P(y, z)P(z, x) = P(x, z)P(z, y)P(y, x).$$

PROOF.   Observe that if $T = \{x, y, z\}$,

$$\frac{P_T(x)}{P_T(y)} \frac{P_T(y)}{P_T(z)} \frac{P_T(z)}{P_T(x)} = 1.$$

Thus, by lemma 3,

$$\frac{P(x, y)}{P(y, x)} \frac{P(y, z)}{P(z, y)} \frac{P(z, x)}{P(x, z)} = 1.$$

Corollary. *Under the conditions of the theorem,*

$$P(x, z) = \frac{P(x, y)P(y, z)}{P(x, y)P(y, z) + P(z, y)P(y, x)}.$$

PROOF. Substitute $P(z, x) = 1 - P(x, z)$ in the theorem and solve for $P(x, z)$.

2. Discussion

The major significance of these two theorems will become apparent in what follows; however, one comment upon the second is in order. If each of the pairs from $\{x, y, z\}$ is offered to a subject just once, if his choices are governed by the given probabilities, and if they are statistically independent, then $P(x, y)P(y, z)P(z, x)$ is the probability that his reports form the intransitivity $x > y > z > x$. The second theorem asserts that if axiom 1 holds this probability must be the same as the probability of the reverse intransitivity, namely, $x > z > y > x$.

The primary reason for stating axiom 1 in the form given can now be presented. If it is assumed that part i holds whether or not any pairwise discriminations are perfect, then it is possible to show that theorem 1 also holds without any restrictions. The only problem in doing this is to handle divisions by 0, but with a little care the theorem can be shown to hold. Now, suppose $P(x, z) = 1$ and consider any $y \in U$ such that the modified axiom holds for $T = \{x, y, z\}$. We show, then, that either $P(x, y) = 1$ or $P(y, z) = 1$. Since $P(x, z) = 1$, theorem 1 gives

$$P_T(x) = P(x, y); \qquad P_T(y) = \frac{1}{1 + \dfrac{P(x, y)}{P(y, x)} + \dfrac{P(z, y)}{P(y, z)}}; \qquad P_T(z) = 0.$$

The sum of these three quantities must be 1, which by simple algebra leads to the condition

$$\frac{P(z, y)}{P(y, z)} P(y, x) = 0,$$

provided that $P(x, y) < 1$ is assumed. Therefore, $P(y, z) = 1$.

The essential point, then, is that if we uninhibitedly assume part i of axiom 1 we find that a single case of perfect pairwise discrimination implies that any third alternative is perfectly discriminated relative to at least one of the two original alternatives.   To those familiar with empirical data, such a result will not seem reasonable.   It is difficult to think of, say, a psychophysical continuum in which, by sufficient subdivision, it is not possible ultimately to produce imperfect pairwise discriminations.

One of two tacks can be taken: either modify the axiom to take care of perfect discrimination explicitly or attempt to argue that there are really no cases of perfect discrimination, only apparent ones.   The latter argument can proceed as follows.   Suppose that, with the psychophysicists, we say that alternative y is one just noticeable difference (jnd) "larger" than alternative x when $P(y, x) = \frac{3}{4}$.   Similarly, z is one jnd larger than y, and so two jnds larger than x, when $P(z, y) = \frac{3}{4}$.   And so on.   Consider, now, alternatives a and b where a is n jnds larger than b.   If we assume that all discriminations are imperfect, then by repeatedly applying the corollary of theorem 2 to the alternatives spaced at one-jnd intervals between a and b it is easy to show that $P(a, b) = 1/[1 + (\frac{1}{3})^n]$.   So, for $n = 2$ there is one chance in ten of describing b as larger than a; for $n = 5$ it is already one chance in 244; and for $n = 10$ it is one in 59,050.   Since laboratory estimates of such probabilities are rarely based upon samples larger than several hundred observations, it is highly likely that separations of more than three or four jnds will appear to be perfectly discriminated, even if mathematically they are not.   Indeed, such rare events are not likely to be recorded when observed, the unexpected reversal being attributed to the apparatus or to the experimenter rather than to the subject.

Although all of this has a ring of plausibility, it is far from certain. There are examples, two of which are given below, in which it seems reasonable to suppose that mixed perfect and imperfect discriminations occur.   More important, it is possible in some problems to show that certain reasonable conditions require, as a mathematical matter, that some discriminations be perfect; an example of this may be found in section 3.B. Here we shall be content with the examples.   The first of these, except for minor modifications, is due entirely to Professor John Chipman.[2] Suppose that we have three urns each containing 100 balls, colored black and white.   An event will be the occurrence of a black ball in a random selection from a specified urn, and we will suppose that a subject chooses between urns on the basis of his judgment of the "likelihood" of the events occurring.   He has the following information:

Urn	Information
α	a random sample (replaced) of 10 balls yielded 6 black ones
β	contains 55 black balls
γ	contains 65 black balls

[2] Personal communication.

Because of the different numbers of black balls in these urns it seems plausible that for some subjects $P(\gamma, \beta) = 1$. Equally well, since all that is known about urn α is based upon a single sample of ten, a person is well justified in fearing that it has fewer black balls than β as well as hoping that it has more than γ. If so, we may well find that both

$$P(\gamma, \alpha) < 1 \quad \text{and} \quad P(\alpha, \beta) < 1,$$

which violates the above conclusion, thus casting doubt upon the unrestricted application of part i of axiom 1.

The second example was suggested by Professor William Vickrey.[3] Consider commodity bundles, each of which consists of two components, x and y, which are both perfectly ordered by preference (denoted by $>$). Suppose $x > x'$ and $y > y'$, then it is plausible that $P[(x, y), (x', y')] = 1$. Now choose (x'', y'') such that $x'' > x, x'$ and $y'' < y, y'$ then, at least for some choices, it is plausible that the resulting conflict leads to

$$P[(x, y), (x'', y'')] < 1 \quad \text{and} \quad P[(x'', y''), (x', y')] < 1.$$

Again, if this can actually happen, part i of axiom 1 cannot be assumed when pairwise discriminations are perfect.

3. Coombs' Data

In addition to direct tests of axiom 1, a number of indirect ones are also possible. The first of these arises from the property known as "monotonicity" (Coombs [1958]) or "strong stochastic transitivity" (Davidson and Marschak [1957]), which follows from the corollary to theorem 2. The property is that if $\frac{1}{2} \leqslant P(x, y) < 1$ and $\frac{1}{2} \leqslant P(y, z) < 1$, then $P(x, z) \geqslant P(x, y)$ and $P(x, z) \geqslant P(y, z)$. It is clearly met if $P(x, z) = 1$, so we assume $P(x, z) < 1$. By the corollary to theorem 2,

$$P(x, z) = \frac{P(x, y)P(y, z)}{P(x, y)P(y, z) + P(y, x)P(z, y)}$$

$$= \frac{P(x, y)}{P(x, y) + P(y, x)P(z, y)/P(y, z)}.$$

But since $P(y, z) \geqq \frac{1}{2}$, $P(z, y)/P(y, z) \leqq 1$, and so

$$P(x, z) \geq \frac{P(x, y)}{P(x, y) + P(y, x)}$$

$$= P(x, y).$$

In a similar manner $P(x, z) \geqq P(y, z)$.

[3] At the September 1957 meetings of the Econometric Society.

Coombs [1958] presents preference (for shades of gray) data that appear, at first glance, to reject strong stochastic transitivity: of 120 triples $\{x, y, z\}$ of stimuli, the four subjects exhibited 19, 26, 31, and 58 violations, respectively. There are, however, two questions of interpretation that must be raised. First, the proportions actually compared are, of course, only estimates of the underlying probabilities, and thus, even if the probabilities satisfy strong stochastic transitivity, not all of the proportions can be expected to satisfy it, especially not if, for example, $P(x, y)$ is only slightly less than $P(x, z)$. Fortunately, Coombs reports the proportions, thus making it possible to estimate which violations are significant. A sufficient number seem to be, so this will not explain away his results. Second, the data actually collected were not paired comparisions but the subject's rankings of subsets of four stimuli. The probabilities $P(x, y)$ were then estimated by the number of sets in which x was ranked above y, divided by the total number of sets in which x and y both appeared. As is discussed more fully in section 2.F.2, this proportion need not necessarily be an estimate of $P(x, y)$. For some models that relate the ranking probabilities to the choice probabilities, it is; for others, it is not. It is, therefore, not entirely clear whether or not strong stochastic transitivity has been tested.

Although these observations cast some doubt upon the importance that should be attached to this study, one feature of Coomb's work somewhat tends to undercut these doubts. He presents an a priori argument which leads to the prediction that most of the violations of strong stochastic transitivity should lie within a particular class of triples, and this is rather well sustained by his data. It is clear that the study should be repeated in some fashion using paired comparisions.

E. RATIO SCALE

1. Background

As the study of choice behavior has developed, both in psychology and in economics, one of the central issues that a formal characterization must face are conditions that ensure the existence of a relatively unique numerical scale which in some sense represents the choice behavior of the subjects. Mathematically, the problem is simply one of imposing sufficient axiomatic structure to prove the existence of a scale that is unique up to some group of transformations—the group of positive linear transformations (zero and unit unspecified) has usually been deemed to be just acceptable. These are what Stevens [1951] terms interval scales. But the empirical side-condition that these mathematical assumptions must form a more or less plausible description of human and animal choice behavior has rendered the problem difficult.   There appear to have been three main approaches.

a. **Economics.**   Preference among bundles of goods has been taken to be the underlying primitive in economics, and, as an idealization, it has been assumed to be an algebraic ordering of the commodity bundles. In such models, if any numerical order preserving scale exists, many do. In fact, they are unique only up to monotonic transformations, which renders the numerical character of the scales almost superfluous.   That being so, some economists arrived at the position that it is safer to work only with orderings—as they say, with ordinal utilities in contrast to cardinal[4] ones—and for many of the traditional theorems of economics this is sufficient.   Nonetheless, some work, particularly in modern decision theory, requires cardinal utility scales.   Some extension of the traditional formulation was needed, and a little more than a decade ago it was affected by von Neumann and Morgenstern [1947].   (Actually, Ramsey [1931] suggested some of the same ideas a good deal earlier, but the importance of his work was not recognized until recently.)   Roughly, they continue to suppose that preferences are algebraic, but the domain of choice is extended from a set of "pure alternatives" to the set of all possible gambles that can be generated from the alternatives and an infinite set of chance events.   Preference over these gambles is assumed to meet certain fairly restrictive axioms which, although normatively compelling, seem at best to lack detailed descriptive realism.   Under these conditions, a scale is shown to exist which is unique up to positive linear transformations and which has the important property that the utility of a gamble is equal to the expected utility of its components.

b. **Psychophysics.**   The psychologist has been largely unwilling to make the economist's algebraic idealization, for in some measure the substance of his problem resides in the fact that people are unable to make consistent discriminations.   The early psychophysicists proposed to use these data as a means of scaling subjective sensation.   Ultimately, this question is discussed more fully, mainly because recent workers have tended to reject the earlier ideas, but here it suffices to mention the fact that the attempt was made and that analytical methods were presented to calculate an interval scale whenever certain consistencies are exhibited by the data.   Mathematically, the uniqueness of these scales results in large part from the assumption that the set being scaled is a continuum— a reasonable assumption for such dimensions as sound energy, weight, length, etc.   For a modern discussion of this mathematics, see Luce and Edwards [1958].

[4] Numerical.

c. Psychometrics. In the remainder of psychology a small group of workers, often referred to as psychometricians, have been concerned with scaling objects other than the traditional sensory stimuli. In particular, such concepts as attitude, preference, intelligence, and interest have concerned them. Their problem has in some ways been similar to that confronted by the economists in that scales with appropriate uniqueness properties are hard to come by. The continuous approximation of the psychophysicist was out, and the gambles of the utility theorist—which, in any event, are of dubious realism in many psychological contexts— were not thought of. The resolution arrived at during the second and third decades of this century, largely through the efforts of Thurstone and his students, was roughly this. The, by then, somewhat tarnished psychophysical assumption was taken over that the underlying scale has the property that discrimination between two objects depends upon the numerical difference of their scale values. Since the continuum assumption could not be transferred, this was quite insufficient to lead to a unique scale. Other assumptions had to be added. At the time, statistics was rapidly becoming the somewhat overworked handmaiden of psychology, and normality and independence assumptions were in the wind. With little real justification beyond convenience and need, these were freely introduced until finally adequate uniqueness was achieved. The result: an extensive literature that has been largely ignored by outsiders, who have been uneasy over the strong and none too compelling assumptions employed.

It is true, as Adams and Messick [1957] have recently re-emphasized and spelled out in detail, that the Thurstonian assumptions do lead to testable restrictions on the observables. Nonetheless, it does seem odd first to postulate this rather complex, normally distributed, but unobservable subworld and only then to determine the relations among observables. Are we to believe that our intuitions about the substrata of choice behavior are really as precise as this?

As we shall see, axiom 1 can serve as an alternate foundation for the analysis of choice behavior which, it turns out, imposes substantially the same restrictions upon paired comparisons data as the most widely used of Thurstone's models (see section 2.D.2). However, it is important to recall that Thurstone's constructs can be extended to the analysis of data obtained by category methods, such as equal appearing and successive intervals. Although these models are subject to criticisms in addition to those applicable to his paired comparisons model, they have been widely used with considerable success. To date, no one has suggested a comparable extension of the present theory to deal with category scaling. The difficulty in doing so probably arises, at least in part, from the unresolved conceptual problem discussed in section 1.A.3.

In other areas of choice behavior, specifically motivation and learning, it has been generally assumed that scaling or measurement either is irrelevant or can be indefinitely postponed. Among the exceptional sorties are the papers of Hull et al. [1947] and Young [1947]. However, to one familiar with measurement ideas, the notions òf incentive value and response strength are suggestive of scales.

In all of the fields in which scales have been important they have been constructed under the assumption that only data for pairs of stimuli are known.   In economics this has not been a limitation because of the algebraic nature of their models and the assumed transitivity of preference. In the psychological models, in which discrimination is admittedly not perfect, the pairwise data have not been known to determine choices from larger sets, and the whole problem has remained unresolved.   As we have seen (theorem 1), axiom 1, if accepted, justifies complacency on that score.

The purpose of this section is to show that for situations in which pairwise choice discrimination is imperfect axiom 1 implies the existence of a ratio scale, i.e., one that is unique except for it's unit, independent of any assumptions about the structure of the set of alternatives.   This formulation can be used to solve all of the classical problems in a very simple way.

2. Existence Theorem

Theorem 3. *Suppose that T is a finite subset of U, that $P(x, y) \neq 0, 1$ for all $x, y \in T$, and that axiom 1 holds for T and its subsets, then there exists a positive real-valued function v on T, which is unique up to multiplication by a positive constant, such that for every $S \subset T$*

$$P_S(x) = \frac{v(x)}{\displaystyle\sum_{y \in S} v(y)}.$$

PROOF.   Define $v(x) = kP_T(x)$, where $k > 0$; then by part i of axiom 1 and part iii of the probability axioms we have

$$P_S(x) = \frac{P_T(x)}{P_T(S)}$$

$$= \frac{kP_T(x)}{\displaystyle\sum_{y \in S} kP_T(y)}$$

$$= \frac{v(x)}{\displaystyle\sum_{y \in S} v(y)},$$

so existence is ensured.

To show uniqueness, suppose that v' is another such function; then for any $x \in T$

$$v(x) = kP_T(x) = \frac{kv'(x)}{\sum_{y \in T} v'(y)}.$$

Let $k' = k \Big/ \sum_{y \in T} v'(y)$, and we have $v(x) = k'v'(x)$, which concludes the proof.

In essence, what we have shown is this. If we confine ourselves to a local region T in which all the pairwise discriminations are imperfect, and if the several probability measures are related to one another so that P_S, $S \subset T$, acts like a conditional probability relative to P_T (axiom 1), then the distribution $P_T(x)$ can be interpreted as a particular choice of unit of a ratio scale over T. By itself, this observation seems too trite to warrant comment; however, these local scales can be extended throughout U in a sensible manner which has implications for psychology that seem to have been overlooked.

The practical will note that the v-scale obtained in theorem 3 is not really very useful as it stands for two reasons: (i) the probabilities $P_T(x)$ will be extremely difficult to estimate when T is at all large, and (ii) the scale is defined only over a set having no pairwise perfect discriminations, which is probably only a small portion of any dimension we might wish to scale. The first difficulty is much mitigated when we notice that v can be expressed as

$$v(x) = kP(x, a)/P(a, x),$$

where a is an arbitrary but fixed element of T and k is a positive constant. This follows from the fact that

$$P_T(x) = P_T(a)P(x, a)/P(a, x),$$

according to lemma 3   Thus, if the pairwise probabilities can be estimated sufficiently accurately so that the ratio $P(x, a)/P(a, x)$ is reliable, then v can be determined.

Actually, in practice it would be most ill-advised to estimate the v-scale in this manner because too little of the available data is used. Fortunately, much more efficient—maximum likelihood—estimating schemes are described in the literature (see section 1.E.4 for the references).

3. Extension of v-Scale

For each subset of U in which pairwise discriminations are imperfect the v-scale is defined. Unless we are willing to suppose that in actuality all discriminations are imperfect, we have, at this point, a whole collection of very local scales. These are of interest only if circumstances can be found under which they can be welded together to form a single scale over the whole of U. The basic idea for doing this is simple. If R and S are two sets over which v-scales are defined, and if they overlap, then the arbitrary scale constants are chosen so that the scales coincide over the region of overlap. The problem is to give plausible sufficient conditions so that the extension is possible and unique. These are formulated as two definitions.

Definition 1. *The universal set U with pairwise probabilities $P(x, y)$ is said to be* finitely connected *if for every a, $b \in U$ for which $P(b, a) > \frac{1}{2}$, there exists a finite sequence $x_1, x_2, \cdots, x_n \in U$ such that*

$$\tfrac{1}{2} \leqq P(x_1, a) < 1, \quad \tfrac{1}{2} \leqq P(x_{i+1}, x_i) < 1, \quad \text{and} \quad \tfrac{1}{2} \leqq P(b, x_n) < 1,$$

where $i = 1, 2, \cdots, n - 1$.

Intuitively, this definition means that any two stimuli are connected via a finite chain of imperfect discriminations. For all practical purposes this condition is met by every psychophysical continuum, and it is probably suitable for other domains provided that we are not too niggardly in defining U.

The next definition has been suggested by Marschak and others (Block and Marschak [1957] and Davidson and Marschak [1958]), and they have studied some of its relations to other concepts.

Definition 2. *The universal set U with pairwise probabilities $P(x, y)$ is said to satisfy the condition of* strong stochastic transitivity *if for every $x, y, z \in U$ such that $P(x, y) \geqq \frac{1}{2}$ and $P(y, z) \geqq \frac{1}{2}$ then $P(x, z) \geqq max\,[P(x, y), P(y, z)]$.*

It is clear that if all pairwise discriminations are imperfect the first definition is satisfied. If all pairwise discriminations are imperfect, and if axiom 1 holds for all sets of three elements, then the second is also met, as was shown in 1.D.3.

Theorem 4. *Suppose that P_T is defined for every $T \subset U$ such that $|T| \leqq 3$, that axiom 1 holds for such sets, that U is finitely connected, and that the condition of strong stochastic transitivity is met. Then there exists a positive ratio scale v on U such that for every $T \subset U$ for which part i of axiom 1 holds*

$$P_T(x) = \frac{v(x)}{\displaystyle\sum_{y \in T} v(y)}.$$

PROOF. Choose any $a \in U$ and set $v(a) = k$, where k is a fixed positive number. Consider any other $b \in U$. If $P(a, b) = \frac{1}{2}$, set $v(b) = k$. If $P(b, a) > \frac{1}{2}$, then by finite connectivity there exists a sequence $x_1, x_2, \cdots, x_n \in U$ forming a chain of imperfect discriminations from a to b.

Set

$$v(b) = k \frac{P(x_1, a)P(x_2, x_1) \cdots P(x_n, x_{n-1})P(b, x_n)}{P(a, x_1)P(x_1, x_2) \cdots P(x_{n-1}, x_n)P(x_n, b)}.$$

If $P(a, b) > \frac{1}{2}$, then a similar sequence exists from b to a, and the corresponding definition is made.

To complete the proof, it must be shown that the definition is independent of the particular sequence chosen and that for a set of imperfectly discriminated alternatives the definition given here coincides with the v-scale of theorem 3. Let us suppose that $x_1, x_2, \cdots, x_n$ and $y_1, y_2, \cdots, y_m$ are two suitable sequences from a to b, where, with no loss of generality, $P(b, a) > \frac{1}{2}$. Now, either $P(x_1, y_1) \geqq \frac{1}{2}$ or $< \frac{1}{2}$. Suppose, again with no loss of generality, that the former holds. By strong stochastic transitivity,

$$P(x_1, y_1) \leqq P(x_1, a) < 1,$$

so by applying theorem 2 to $\{a, x_1, y_1\}$ we have

$$\frac{P(x_1, a)}{P(a, x_1)} = \frac{P(x_1, y_1)P(y_1, a)}{P(y_1, x_1)P(a, y_1)}.$$

Because

$$v(y_1) = k \frac{P(y_1, a)}{P(a, y_1)},$$

it follows that

$$k \frac{P(x_1, a)}{P(a, x_1)} = k \frac{P(x_1, y_1)P(y_1, a)}{P(y_1, x_1)P(c, y_1)}$$

$$= v(y_1) \frac{P(x_1, y_1)}{P(y_1, x_1)}.$$

Thus, we can begin the argument at y_1 rather than at a. Proceeding inductively, we can continue to move the starting point through the finite number of elements up to b, in which case uniqueness is trivial.

If $b, c \in U$ are such that $\frac{1}{2} \leqq P(c, b) < 1$ and if $v(b)$ is defined in terms of the sequence $x_1, x_2, \cdots, x_n$, then we may define $v(c)$ in terms of the sequence $x_1, x_2, \cdots, x_n, b$. Thus

$$\frac{v(c)}{v(b)} = \frac{P(c, b)}{P(b, c)}$$

because k and all the x_i terms are common to both definitions and so they cancel. This establishes the compatibility of the present scale with the one discussed in theorem 3, hence proving the final assertion of the present theorem.

The role of finite connectedness is to permit an extension of v throughout all of U, and the role of strong stochastic transitivity is to ensure one dimensionality and, thus, a unique extension of v. It should be pointed out that we do not need quite so strong a condition as definition 2; it would suffice to demand that if $P(x, y) \geqq \frac{1}{2}$, $P(y, z) \geqq \frac{1}{2}$, and $P(x, z) < 1$ then $P(x, y) < 1$ and $P(y, z) < 1$.

One important practical consequence of this theorem is that axiom 1 need hold only for subsets of three alternatives in order for the v-scale to exist. Thus any proposed counter example to axiom 1 will be of interest only if it is based on sets of three alternatives.

Another fact brought out by the theorem is that although axiom 1 implies unidimensionality when pairwise discrimination is perfect throughout (lemma 4) or when it is imperfect throughout (theorem 3) other restrictions must be added to axiom 1 to get unidimensionality when there are mixed perfect and imperfect pairwise discriminations. In the mixed case axiom 1 amounts to an assumption of local linearity. This strongly suggests that axiom 1 by itself admits a multidimensional scaling model when discriminations are mixed; however I have not yet been able to construct such a model.

4. Previous Work

The hypothesis that a numerical scale v might exist such that

$$P_T(x) = \frac{v(x)}{\displaystyle\sum_{y \in T} v(y)}$$

has appeared, at least for paired comparisons, from time to time in the literature as an *ad hoc* assumption. For example, Thurstone [1930] and, following him, Gulliksen [1953] postulated this in a learning theory in which v was interpreted as "response strength" (see Chapter 4). Undoubtedly it has appeared in other specific applications.

Of much greater importance, however, is the existence of a relatively extensive statistical literature based upon the two alternative version of this model. For a number of years R. A. Bradley has championed the assumption for paired comparisons data that $P(x, y) = v(x)/[v(x) + v(y)]$, and he and various colleagues have developed methods for estimating the scale values and for testing certain statistical hypotheses. The existence of their work, which complements the theoretical work described here and which is of utmost importance for empirical applications of the model, means that the statistical aspects of the present theory are much better understood than one would have any reason to hope a priori.

Since these developments are generally available, there is no need to summarize them except to indicate briefly what has been done. Bradley and Terry [1952] present maximum likelihood estimates for the v's in the paired comparisons case, and they develop several likelihood ratio tests for the null hypothesis that all of the v's are the same.   Asymptotic results are obtained, and tables are included of the maximum likelihood estimates and the test statistics for small sample sizes.   These tables are extended in Bradley [1954a].   In Bradley [1955] the power of the tests and the reliability of the estimators are studied.   An extension of these methods to treatments that form a factorial set in paired comparisons is presented by Abelson and Bradley [1954].   Independently of this work, Ford [1957] has discussed the maximum likelihood estimates of the v's for the same model with, however, the generalization that the sample size may differ from pair to pair.   Finally, in Bradley [1954b] the goodness of fit of the underlying model is discussed.   He develops a test statistic having the χ^2 distribution for large sample sizes, which he shows is approximately the same as the ordinary test statistic based upon expected frequencies calculated from the maximum likelihood estimates.   Twenty tests of the model, based upon data from two experiments, are given, and only one χ^2 is significant at the 0.05 level.   In addition, Bradley refers to unpublished work of J. W. Hopkins in which extensive tests of the model have been conducted on taste sensations; he reports that these data give no reason to reject the model.

F. INDEPENDENCE-OF-UNIT CONDITION

1. Statement of Condition

In this section a condition about theory construction is developed that limits significantly the possible form that certain theories based on axiom 1 can assume.   This condition must, I believe, be classed as extra-empirical, since it is intended to capture in part what we mean by an acceptable theory.   Its application is not restricted to situations in which axiom 1 is assumed but holds whenever one or more of the variables involved form ratio scales.   Since arguments of the type to be used have not often occurred in the behavioral sciences and may, therefore, seem suspect to some, it should be pointed out that they have adequate precedent from physics.   For example, the condition that the laws of physics should be independent of translations and rotations of the coordinate system within which they are stated seems innocent enough, but it limits appreciably the possible physical laws.   It is a condition about the nature of theory and the use of the word law, not an empirical hypothesis.

After discussing the condition and an empirical assumption, we will see how they may be used to analyze a problem of some inherent interest: the time- and space-order effects.   Later they reappear in the analysis of the signal detectability problem (section 2.E) and of learning (Chapter 4).

By definition, a ratio scale is specified except for its unit, which is not only unknown but unknowable. The unit is a matter of convention. Therefore, it seems illegitimate, if not actually inconsistent, for a theory to presuppose that the unit is known. And so, in its most general form, the condition to be imposed is that *any theory involving a ratio scale shall be independent of the unit chosen for that scale.* Indeed, if this were not so, empirical observations determining the form of the theory would permit us to evaluate the unit, and so the scale would be stronger than a ratio scale.

This condition must now be made specific to the present choice problem. Suppose, for example, that theorem 4 holds for choice probabilities over a set U of alternatives both before and after the occurrence of some event which is relevant to the organism making the choice. The event might be some physical stimulus in a psychophysical experiment, or it might be the occurrence of reward in a learning experiment, etc. In general, an event may be thought of as effecting a change of state in the organism. The scale values in one state come about as a modification, due to the event, of those that existed in the other state. It is appropriate to think in terms of states rather than events, even though only the latter interpretation is used in this book, because the general principle is concerned with the effect of different determiners of behavior upon the scale values, not just temporal events. Let us consider theories in which the scale value for alternative $x \in U$ is dependent upon only three things when the organism is in the state S_2: the states S_1 and S_2 and the scale value in S_1. Thus there is no loss of generality in writing the transformed value as $f[v(x)]$, where $v(x)$ is the scale value for state S_1 and f is a function which depends only upon x and the states S_1 and S_2. The condition, then, says that the mathematical form of f shall not depend upon our choice of unit, which is to say that if v transforms into $f(v)$ for a particular unit, and if we change the unit by multiplying throughout by a positive constant k, then kv must be transformed into $kf(v)$. In summary, we may state the condition as follows:

Independence-of-unit condition.

Suppose that the choice probabilities of an organism over subsets of U satisfy the conditions of theorem 4 both when the organism is in state S_1 and when it is in state S_2. Suppose, further, that the scale values for $x \in U$ can be written as $v(x)$ and $[v(x)]$ for S_1 and S_2, respectively, where f is a function that depends only upon x, S_1, and S_2. Then, for any $k > 0$

$$f[kv(x)] = kf[v(x)].$$

2. Behavioral Continuity

Although the point is rarely raised, implicit in most scaling theories is the assumption that any real number can appear as a scale value. Certainly, the evidence has not been so overwhelming that theorists have been forced to assume otherwise.   Nonetheless, it is an assumption that may in fact be false, and some have felt, in particular, that an unbounded v-scale is counter intuitive.   As we shall see later, when we study learning models, the assumption of a bounded v-scale leads us to certain peculiar results.   So let us tentatively impose the following assumption:

Unboundedness assumption.

Any positive real number is a possible value on the v-scale.

The independence-of-unit condition, together with the unboundedness assumption, determines explicitly the form of the transformation f, since by the unboundedness assumption the number 1 is a possible scale value whatever the unit may be, and so, by the independence-of-unit condition

$$f(v) = f(v1)$$
$$= vf(1).$$

This is to say, the only admissible transformations of the v's are multiplications by positive constants (positive because $f(1)$ must be a scale value). It is useful to replace $f(1)$ by a symbol which makes its dependencies explicit, e.g., α_{ix}, where i refers to the event that effects the transition from one state to another and x refers to the alternative.

3. Response Bias

The essential feature of any experiment in which the so-called time- or space-order errors appear is this.   The subject is confronted by several stimuli that he is to rank according to some intrinsic but, to him, ambiguous property.   Each stimulus is temporarily identified by some unambiguous label that is accessible both to the subject and to the experimenter and that is unrelated to the property the subject is judging.   For example, if the stimuli are weights of nearly the same mass, the property to be judged can be relative heaviness and the temporary labels can be their serial positions in the order of lifting.   Or, if the stimuli are patches of light to be judged according to relative brightness, then their location in space can be used as the temporary identifying label.   Other identifications can be used so long as they are not correlated with the dimension being judged.   It is a priori clear that however the objects may be labeled the subject may exhibit a bias among the labeling categories; it is doubtful that the bias really has much to do with space or time or order, and so following Irwin [1958] the more neutral term *response bias* is used.

Whatever it is called, the bias occurs and must be coped with in some manner—and the obvious idea of randomizing it out of existence only muddies the data beyond use. The analysis that is to be proposed is most easily illustrated by a specific example; once that is understood, the generalizations will be obvious. Let the stimuli be three weights called H, M, and L (for heavy, medium, and light). These are presented sequentially, and the subject identifies the one that he thinks is heaviest by saying whether it was the first, second, or third presented. The data table consists of six rows, one for each of the orders HML, HLM, etc., and three columns, one for each of the response categories.

Prior to hefting the weights, a certain differential tendency to use the categories may be assumed to exist. Let the corresponding v-values be v_1, v_2, and v_3. After lifting the weights, these tendencies will be altered, and, if we are willing to suppose that the modification depends only upon the weights lifted, their order, and the value of the response category, then the independence-of-unit condition and the unboundedness assumption imply that the effect will be multiplicative. Thus the three v-values in row i may be written as

$$\alpha_{i1}v_1, \qquad \alpha_{i2}v_2, \quad \text{and} \quad \alpha_{i3}v_3.$$

Although it may be that the effect upon each response category depends upon all three of the weights, it would be much simpler if there were no interaction. Assuming this is so, then the effect actually depends only upon the weight that happens to correspond to that category. Thus there are only three parameters, say α corresponding to H, β to M, and γ to L. The model may then be summarized as

$$
\begin{array}{c@{\qquad}ccc}
 & 1 & 2 & 3 \\
HML & \alpha v_1 & \beta v_2 & \gamma v_3 \\
HLM & \alpha v_1 & \gamma v_2 & \beta v_3 \\
MHL & \beta v_1 & \alpha v_2 & \gamma v_3 \\
LHM & \gamma v_1 & \alpha v_2 & \beta v_3 \\
MLH & \beta v_1 & \gamma v_2 & \alpha v_3 \\
LMH & \gamma v_1 & \beta v_2 & \alpha v_3 \\
\end{array}.
$$

Assuming imperfect discrimination, the probabilities in each row are determined according to theorem 4 by the values in each row. For example, the probabilities in the HLM row are

$$\frac{\alpha v_1}{\alpha v_1 + \gamma v_2 + \beta v_3}, \qquad \frac{\gamma v_2}{\alpha v_1 + \gamma v_2 + \beta v_3}, \qquad \frac{\beta v_3}{\alpha v_1 + \gamma v_2 + \beta v_3}.$$

Since the unit in each row may be changed without affecting the probabilities, the entire table may be divided by γv_1, yielding

$$\begin{bmatrix} \dfrac{\alpha}{\gamma} & \dfrac{\beta\,v_2}{\gamma\,v_1} & \dfrac{v_3}{v_1} \\[2ex] \dfrac{\alpha}{\gamma} & \dfrac{v_2}{v_1} & \dfrac{\beta\,v_3}{\gamma\,v_1} \\[2ex] \dfrac{\beta}{\gamma} & \dfrac{\alpha\,v_2}{\gamma\,v_1} & \dfrac{v_3}{v_1} \\[2ex] 1 & \dfrac{\alpha\,v_2}{\gamma\,v_1} & \dfrac{\beta\,v_3}{\gamma\,v_1} \\[2ex] \dfrac{\beta}{\gamma} & \dfrac{v_2}{v_1} & \dfrac{\alpha\,v_3}{\gamma\,v_1} \\[2ex] 1 & \dfrac{\beta\,v_2}{\gamma\,v_1} & \dfrac{\alpha\,v_3}{\gamma\,v_1} \end{bmatrix}.$$

This, in turn, can be decomposed by matrix multiplication into

$$\begin{bmatrix} \dfrac{\alpha}{\gamma} & \dfrac{\beta}{\gamma} & 1 \\[2ex] \dfrac{\alpha}{\gamma} & 1 & \dfrac{\beta}{\gamma} \\[2ex] \dfrac{\beta}{\gamma} & \dfrac{\alpha}{\gamma} & 1 \\[2ex] 1 & \dfrac{\alpha}{\gamma} & \dfrac{\beta}{\gamma} \\[2ex] \dfrac{\beta}{\gamma} & 1 & \dfrac{\alpha}{\gamma} \\[2ex] 1 & \dfrac{\beta}{\gamma} & \dfrac{\alpha}{\gamma} \end{bmatrix} \begin{bmatrix} 1 & 0 & 0 \\[2ex] 0 & \dfrac{v_2}{v_1} & 0 \\[2ex] 0 & 0 & \dfrac{v_3}{v_1} \end{bmatrix}.$$

Observe that there are really only four parameters, not six, in this model. If four stimuli are used, the generalization is clear: there are 24 rows, four columns, and six parameters. And so on. In this fashion it is clear that we can separate out the so-called time- or space-order errors, making it possible to use psychophysical data to check axiom 1.

4. Estimation of Parameters

To apply this model, it is necessary to estimate the several parameters from data. No work has been done on optimal estimation methods, but the following technique has been used with success. Its main virtue is algebraic simplicity.

Let P_{ij} denote the probability corresponding to the ith row and the jth column, and let $A_{ijk} = P_{ij}/P_{ik}$. Then the three-stimulus model implies the following matrix:

$$
\begin{array}{c}
 & A_{i12} & A_{i13} & A_{i23} \\
HML & \begin{bmatrix} \dfrac{\alpha\,v_1}{\beta\,v_2} & \dfrac{\alpha\,v_1}{\gamma\,v_3} & \dfrac{\beta\,v_2}{\gamma\,v_3} \end{bmatrix} \\
HLM & \begin{bmatrix} \dfrac{\alpha\,v_1}{\gamma\,v_2} & \dfrac{\alpha\,v_1}{\beta\,v_3} & \dfrac{\gamma\,v_2}{\beta\,v_3} \end{bmatrix} \\
MHL & \begin{bmatrix} \dfrac{\beta\,v_1}{\alpha\,v_2} & \dfrac{\beta\,v_1}{\gamma\,v_3} & \dfrac{\alpha\,v_2}{\gamma\,v_3} \end{bmatrix} \\
LHM & \begin{bmatrix} \dfrac{\gamma\,v_1}{\alpha\,v_2} & \dfrac{\gamma\,v_1}{\beta\,v_3} & \dfrac{\alpha\,v_2}{\beta\,v_3} \end{bmatrix} \\
MLH & \begin{bmatrix} \dfrac{\beta\,v_1}{\gamma\,v_2} & \dfrac{\beta\,v_1}{\alpha\,v_3} & \dfrac{\gamma\,v_2}{\alpha\,v_3} \end{bmatrix} \\
LMH & \begin{bmatrix} \dfrac{\gamma\,v_1}{\beta\,v_2} & \dfrac{\gamma\,v_1}{\alpha\,v_3} & \dfrac{\beta\,v_2}{\alpha\,v_3} \end{bmatrix}
\end{array}
$$

It is easy to see that

$$\frac{\alpha}{\beta} = \left(\frac{A_{112}A_{213}A_{423}}{A_{312}A_{513}A_{623}} \right)^{\frac{1}{6}}$$

$$\frac{\beta}{\gamma} = \left(\frac{A_{512}A_{313}A_{123}}{A_{612}A_{413}A_{223}} \right)^{\frac{1}{6}}$$

$$\frac{\alpha}{\gamma} = \left(\frac{A_{212}A_{113}A_{323}}{A_{412}A_{613}A_{523}} \right)^{\frac{1}{6}}$$

$$\frac{v_1}{v_2} = \left(\prod_{i=1}^{6} A_{i12} \right)^{\frac{1}{6}}$$

$$\frac{v_1}{v_3} = \left(\prod_{i=1}^{6} A_{i13} \right)^{\frac{1}{6}}$$

$$\frac{v_2}{v_3} = \left(\prod_{i=1}^{6} A_{i23} \right)^{\frac{1}{6}}$$

As a computational check, it is not difficult to show that the following equations must hold:

$$\left(\frac{\hat{\alpha}}{\beta}\right)\left(\frac{\hat{\beta}}{\gamma}\right)\Big/\left(\frac{\hat{\alpha}}{\gamma}\right) = 1$$

$$\left(\frac{\hat{v}_1}{v_2}\right)\left(\frac{\hat{v}_2}{v_3}\right)\Big/\left(\frac{\hat{v}_1}{v_3}\right) = 1.$$

G. ALGEBRAIC APPROXIMATIONS[5]

As pointed out in section 1.A.1, there is some disagreement as to whether an algebraic or probabilistic description of choice behavior is to be preferred. One argument favoring the algebraic approach is the apparent greater simplicity of the resulting mathematics, and some would hold that even if the probabilistic model were more accurate it should, nonetheless, be replaced by some algebraic approximation. In this section the properties of two such approximations to the pairwise discriminations are examined when axiom 1 is assumed to hold for sets of three alternatives.

1. Just Noticeable Differences

The most ancient and honorable, if frequently misunderstood, technique for passing from a probabilistic to an algebraic model is to introduce the concept of a just noticeable difference (jnd). This has been widely employed in psychophysics; however, there is no particular reason to restrict it to any special class of choice phenomena. The essential idea is to pick a probability cutoff π, $\frac{1}{2} < \pi < 1$, and to say that alternatives discriminated more than 100π per cent of the time are more than one jnd apart; those discriminated less often are one jnd or less apart. This can be cast in the language of binary relations as follows:

Definition 3. *Suppose that for every* $x, y \in U$, $P(x, y)$ *is defined, and let* π *be a fixed number,* $\frac{1}{2} < \pi < 1$. *The relation* $L(\pi)$ *on* U *is defined by* $xL(\pi)y$ *if and only if* $P(x, y) > \pi$. *The relation* $I(\pi)$ *on* U *is defined by* $xI(\pi)y$ *if and only if* $1 - \pi \leqq P(x, y) \leqq \pi$.

The intuitive meaning of $L(\pi)$ is "at least one π-jnd larger" and of $I(\pi)$, "not more than one π-jnd apart." It is, of course, necessary to specify the value of π, since these relations change with changes in π. That is to say, it is meaningless to speak of jnds without specifying the probability cutoff that was used to define them—a point unfortunately all too often ignored in the experimental literature.

[5] This section is included for completeness, but it is not necessary in order to understand any of the following work.

The question is what properties—axioms—these relations can be expected to meet. We might well expect $L(\pi)$ to be transitive—that when x is at least one jnd larger than y and y at least one jnd larger than z then x should be at least one jnd larger than z. On the other hand, we definitely do not expect $I(\pi)$ to be transitive. In Luce [1956] this question was treated abstractly in terms of conditions that two such relations might be expected to satisfy, and the following axiom system was offered:

Semiorder axioms. *Let L and I be binary relations on a set U. (L, I) is said to be a semiordering of U if for every $x, y, z, w \in U$*

(i) exactly one of xLy, yLx, or xIy obtains,
(ii) xIx,
(iii) xLy, yIz, zLw imply xLw,
(iv) xLy and yLz imply not both xIw and wIz.

Theorem 5. *Let T be any subset of U in which all pairwise discriminations are imperfect; suppose that P_S is defined for every $S \subset T$ such that $|S| \leq 3$; and suppose that for these subsets axiom 1 holds. Then for each π, $\frac{1}{2} < \pi < 1$, the relations $L(\pi)$ and $I(\pi)$ form a semiordering of T.*

PROOF. By theorem 4, there exists a scale v on T such that

$$P(x, y) = v(x)/[v(x) + v(y)]$$
$$= 1/[1 + v(y)/v(x)].$$

Thus $xL(\pi)y$ if and only if $1/[1 + v(y)/v(x)] > \pi$, which is equivalent to $v(x)/v(y) > \pi/(1 - \pi)$. Similarly, $xI(\pi)y$ if and only if $(1 - \pi)/\pi \leq v(x)/v(y) \leq \pi/(1 - \pi)$. Now the four semiorder axioms can be checked. The first two are trivial. The hypotheses of the third amount to

$$v(x)/v(y) > \pi/(1 - \pi), \qquad (1 - \pi)/\pi \leq v(y)/v(z) \leq \pi/(1 - \pi),$$
$$v(z)/v(w) > \pi/(1 - \pi).$$

Thus

$$\frac{v(x)}{v(w)} = \frac{v(x)}{v(y)} \frac{v(y)}{v(z)} \frac{v(z)}{v(w)}$$

$$> \frac{\pi}{(1 - \pi)} \frac{(1 - \pi)}{\pi} \frac{\pi}{(1 - \pi)}$$

$$= \frac{\pi}{1 - \pi},$$

as was to be shown. Suppose in the fourth axiom that $xI(\pi)w$, then we show $wL(\pi)z$. The hypotheses amount to

$$v(x)/v(y) > \pi/(1 - \pi), \qquad v(y)/v(z) > \pi/(1 - \pi),$$

$$(1 - \pi)/\pi \leqq v(x)/v(w) \leqq \pi/(1 - \pi).$$

Thus

$$\frac{v(w)}{v(z)} = \frac{v(y)}{v(z)} \frac{v(x)}{v(y)} \frac{v(w)}{v(x)}$$

$$> \frac{\pi}{(1 - \pi)} \frac{\pi}{(1 - \pi)} \frac{(1 - \pi)}{\pi}$$

$$= \frac{\pi}{1 - \pi},$$

which concludes the proof.

If we wish to treat two alternatives that are less than one jnd apart as being, in a sense, indifferent, then the foregoing algebraic system seems to be appropriate. It is, however, in some ways more difficult to work with than the one to be described next.

2. The Trace

In most of the algebraic models of choice it has been customary to work with weak orderings which have the important property that the indifference relation is transitive.

Weak order axioms. *Let R be a binary relation on a set U. R is said to be a weak ordering of U if for every $x, y, z \in U$*

(i) *either xRy or yRx or both,*
(ii) *(transitivity) xRy and yRz imply xRz.*

By defining xLy to mean xRy but not yRx and xIy to mean both xRy and yRx, it is not difficult to show that (L, I) satisfies the semiorder axioms; however, I is also transitive.

The importance of weak orders stems mainly from the fact that if v is a numerical mapping of U that preserves the order of a binary relation R on U, i.e.,

$$v(x) \geqq v(y) \text{ if and only if } xRy,$$

then R must be a weak ordering of U.

The problem now is whether there is a weak order that approximates a probabilistic model. As shown in Luce [1956], every semiorder induces a natural weak order, so from theorem 5 we know that if axiom 1 holds we can induce an infinity of weak orders, one for each value of π. These, however, are less interesting and less refined in a sense than the following relation defined in Luce [1958].

Definition 4. *Suppose that for every* $x, y \in U$, $P(x, y)$ *is defined. The relation* $\gtrsim$ *defined by* $x \gtrsim y$ *if and only if* $P(x, z) \geqq P(y, z)$ *for all* $z \in U$ *is called the* trace *of* P.

It is easy to see that the trace is a transitive relation, but without some restrictions on P it need not be a weak order. That is, there may exist incomparable pairs (x, y) in the sense that z and $z' \in U$ can be found such that $P(x, z) > P(y, z)$ and $P(x, z') < P(y, z')$. Unfortunately, we cannot show that the trace is a weak order under exactly the same conditions employed in theorem 5 because, unlike the relations $L(\pi)$ and $I(\pi)$ which are defined just in terms of the probabilities of two alternatives, the trace depends upon the relation of x and y to all other alternatives in U.

Theorem 6. *Suppose that* P_S *is defined for every subset* $S \subset U$ *such that* $|S| \leqq 3$, *that axiom 1 holds for such sets, and that all pairwise discriminations are imperfect. Then the trace is a weak order.*

PROOF. By definition of the trace, $x \gtrsim y$ if and only if $P(x, z) \geqq P(y, z)$, $z \in U$. Since imperfect discrimination and axiom 1 imply strong stochastic transitivity, theorem 4 holds, and so the preceding condition is equivalent to

$$\frac{v(x)}{v(x) + v(z)} \geqq \frac{v(y)}{v(y) + v(z)},$$

which in turn is equivalent to $v(x) \geqq v(y)$. Thus, for every $x, y \in U$, either $x > y$ or $y \gtrsim x$, as was to be shown.

Corollary. *Under the conditions of the theorem,* $x \gtrsim y$ *if and only if* $P(x, y)$ $\geqq \frac{1}{2}$.

PROOF. Obvious.

This theorem can also be shown as follows: as noted in section 1.E.3, the hypotheses imply the condition of strong stochastic transitivity, and Block and Marschak [1957] have shown this condition to be equivalent to the trace being a weak order.

chapter 2

Applications
to Psychophysics

A. FECHNER'S PROBLEM

1. The Fechnerian Assumption

One way of describing part of the content of theorem 4 is to say that when pairwise discriminations are imperfect axiom 1 is sufficient to render the discrimination problem mathematically one-dimensional. This is most vivid for the pairwise discriminations for which

$$P(x, y) = \frac{1}{1 + v(y)/v(x)}.$$

The idea that discrimination along a single sensory continuum might be mathematically one-dimensional has long been common in psychology. It was first postulated by Fechner in psychophysics, and it has been widely assumed there and elsewhere, but without an axiomatic justification such as has been given here. As Fechner's assumption has been the subject of a good deal of discussion and controversy in psychology, and as many psychologists now reject what is often called the Fechnerian position, it is important to examine what is involved in some detail.

It is generally held that Fechner assumed the subjective sensation of intensity arising from stimuli which lie on a physical continuum to be given by that transformation of the physical continuum which renders discrimination dependent only upon sensation differences.[1] This is now believed on empirical grounds to be wrong (see Stevens [1957]). It seems to me that whether or not his assumption can be rejected greatly depends upon exactly what it is, and about this there is some confusion. There are two quite distinct parts to it:

(i) The probabilities of pairwise discriminations, the $P(x, y)$, are so constrained that there exists a real-valued mapping u of the stimuli and a function F of one real variable such that, for $P(x, y) \neq 0$ or 1, $P(x, y) = F[u(x) - u(y)]$.

(ii) The function u of part i represents "subjective sensation."

Now, although part i must be true for part ii to have any meaning at all, the truth or falsity of part ii, however it may be interpreted, asserts nothing at all about the truth or falsity of part i. This simple point seems to have been slurred over a good deal in the discussions of Fechner's assumption(s).

Psychologists have interpreted part ii as implying various reasonable things about behavior, and these implications have turned out empirically to be false. For example, let x and y be two soft tones and x' and y' two loud tones, all of the same frequency such that $u(x) - u(y) = u(x') - u(y')$. It is argued that if u really represents subjective sensation the two differences should seem to be of the same size to subjects; they do not. For such reasons the Fechnerian position has been rejected—not just part ii but also part i. It would appear that part i should be dealt with separately and, if true, retained, since the reduction of an apparently multidimensional phenomenon to a single dimension is an achievement not to be lightly discarded.

2. Derivation of Fechner's Assumption

Part of the reason for rejecting part i as well as part ii, even though the evidence does not force us to do so, doubtless is the fact that the restriction is difficult to accept as a primitive axiom. Somehow it is much too sophisticated and not sufficiently compelling to be treated other than as an interesting conjecture. What has been lacking is a basic axiom system from which it would follow as a consequence.

In axiom 1, however, we have a condition that is sufficient to prove

---

[1] Most often Fechner's assumption is phrased in terms of the equality of sensation jnds, and the stated postulate is referred to as the principle that "equally often noticed differences are equal, unless always or never noticed." Of course, the jnd concept is actually an algebraic construct from statistical data, and it is not surprising to find that the two are actually the same assumption. A full discussion of this point will be found in Luce and Edwards [1958].

Fechner's assumption i when discrimination is imperfect and to do so quite generally without restricting U to be a continuum. This is easily seen by setting

$$u = \frac{1}{k} \log v + a,$$

where $k > 0$, in which case theorem 4 implies

$$P(x, y) = \frac{1}{1 + \dfrac{v(y)}{v(x)}}$$

$$= \frac{1}{1 + \dfrac{\exp \{k[u(y) - a]\}}{\exp \{k[u(x) - a]\}}}$$

$$= \frac{1}{1 + \exp \{-k[u(x) - u(y)]\}}.$$

For obvious reasons, log v will be referred to as the *Fechnerian scale*.

The above discrimination function is known as the logistic curve. In shape it is extremely similar to the integral of the normal curve, and from time to time it has been proposed as a possible approximation for dis-

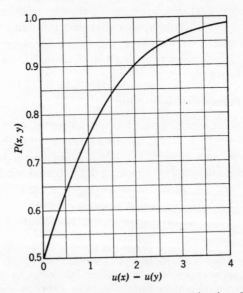

Figure 2. The logistic curve with the normalization $P(x, y) = 0.75$ when $u(x) - u(y) = 1$.

crimination data (see Guilford [1954], p. 144).   In Figure 2 the curve is plotted with the normalization that when $u(x) - u(y) = 1$ then $P(x, y) = 0.75$ (which corresponds to defining one jnd by a 0.75 probability cutoff). The relation of the logistic to the integral of the normal distribution is discussed in section 2.D.2.

It appears that v is a much more basic scale than Fechner's.   For example, v relates to the probabilities in a particularly simple way, making the calculations of $P_T(S)$ almost trivial (theorem 4), and it is a ratio scale, whereas u is only an interval scale.   In most of the following applications v appears to play a more central role than log v.   Nonetheless, if axiom 1 holds, Fechner was correct in the first half of his assumption, though he need not have confined his conjecture to stimuli from physical continua.

Recently, Stevens [1957] has argued on empirical grounds that it is indeed true that discrimination is mathematically one-dimensional but that it depends upon ratios of scale values, not differences as assumed by Fechner.   This is, of course, what we have shown must hold for the v-scale; in addition, the results in section 2.B show other strong correspondences between our scale and the one Stevens has discussed.

3. Uniqueness of the Logistic Curve

One might imagine that there are transformations of the v-scale other than the logarithm that solve Fechner's problem; however, Adams and Messick [1957] have shown that it is unique for psychophysical continua, though not necessarily for other domains for which the image of the scale is a proper subset of the reals.   With their kind permission, their proof is reproduced here.   Suppose that

$$\frac{v(x)}{v(x) + v(y)} = F[u(x) - u(y)],$$

where F is a monotonic increasing function.   By holding y fixed, it is clear that $v(x)$ is a monotonic increasing function of $u(x)$, say $v(x) = g[u(x)]$.   Now, if we suppose that for every real number r there exists some $x \in U$ such that $r = u(x)$, the equation can be written

$$\frac{g(r)}{g(r) + g(s)} = F[r - s],$$

for every real r and s.   But

$$\frac{g(r - s)}{g(r - s) + g(0)} = F(r - s)$$

$$= \frac{g(r)}{g(r) + g(s)},$$

and clearing fractions and writing $t = r - s$ we have

$$g(s)g(t) = g(0)g(s + t).$$

Let $h(s) = \log g(s) - \log g(0)$; then the above equation reduces to

$$h(s + t) = h(s) + h(t).$$

It is well known that the only monotonic increasing solutions to this functional equation are of the form

$$h(s) = ks,$$

where $k > 0$; so

$$g(s) = g(0)e^{ks}.$$

Thus

$$v(x) = Ce^{ku(x)},$$

and so

$$P(x, y) = \frac{1}{1 + \exp\{-k[u(x) - u(y)]\}},$$

as was to be shown.

B. THE POWER LAW

1. Derivation of the Law

If, with the psychophysicists, we reject Fechner's second assumption that $\log v$ represents subjective sensation, then what does? Stevens [1957] and Stevens and Galanter [1957] have reviewed a large aggregate of data which, in part, seems to show that there are at least two quite distinct types of psychophysical continua.

Two general classes of perceptual continua can be distinguished by means of four functional criteria. On Class I or "quantitative" continua the j.n.d. increases in subjective size as psychological magnitude increases, category rating-scales are concave downward when plotted against psychological magnitude, comparative judgments exhibit a time-order error (a "category effect"), and equisection experiments exhibit hysteresis. On Class II or "qualitative" continua these four effects are apparently absent. Class I, called prothetic, includes those continua on which discrimination is mediated by an additive mechanism at the physiological level; Class II, called metathetic, includes those mediated by a substitutive mechanism.

On Class I (prothetic) continua the use of one or more of four kinds of direct methods for constructing ratio scales reveals that equal stimulus ratios tend to produce equal subjective ratios. Hence, to a first-order approximation the "psychophysical law" relating stimulus and response is a power function. The exponent, as measured on fourteen different continua, varies from about 0.3 for loudness to about 2.0 for visual flash rate. (Stevens [1957], p. 178.)

Furthermore, (pairwise) discrimination on prothetic continua[2] is approximately proportional to physical intensity (Weber's law[3]), or more precisely (see Miller [1947]) it is linear with intensity. Yet, as indicated by Stevens, when a person is asked to assign numbers to the stimuli so that they are proportional to subjective magnitudes (the method of magnitude estimation), the data can usually be fitted quite accurately by a power function Ax^B, where B is a constant between 0.3 and 4 or 5, depending upon the continuum[4] and provided that it is measured in ordinary physical units (see Stevens [1957]).

Let us suppose that axiom 1 holds, that the v-scale is a continuous function of physical intensity, and that prothetic continua are characterized by the property that the linear generalization of Weber's law is true, i.e., given any number π, $\frac{1}{2} < \pi < 1$, there exist numbers $c(\pi)$ and $d(\pi)$ such that

$$P(x, y) = \pi \text{ if and only if } x = [1 + c(\pi)]y + d(\pi).$$

Then we show that

$$v(x) = A[x + C]^B,$$

where

$$A > 0, \qquad B = \frac{\log \pi - \log (1 - \pi)}{\log [1 + c(\pi)]}, \quad \text{and} \quad C = \frac{d(\pi)}{c(\pi)}.$$

Since, by theorem 4,

$$P(x, y) = \frac{v(x)}{v(x) + v(y)},$$

the generalization of Weber's law can be written

$$v\{[1 + c(\pi)]y + d(\pi)\} = \frac{\pi}{(1 - \pi)} v(y).$$

By slightly modifying the results in Luce and Edwards [1958], it can be shown that the solution to this equation is unique except for multiplication by a positive constant, and it is easy to show by substitution that the above v is a solution.

One test of this model which has not been available for earlier ones is its prediction of the form of the discrimination functions. Once B is

[2] Professor Stevens has abandoned the Class I-Class II terminology in favor of prothetic-metathetic because the former generated too much confusion; therefore I shall use the latter.

[3] See the discussion by Householder and Young [1940] of Weber's law.

[4] Since writing the quoted passage, Stevens has studied magnitude estimation of moderate electric shock to the fingers and has found that the exponent is larger than 2. The data are somewhat unstable, but the exponent appears to be about 4 or 5.

determined from π and $c(\pi)$, we predict that

$$P(x, y) = \frac{1}{1 + \left(\dfrac{y + C}{x + C}\right)^B}$$

2. Estimation of Exponent

As far as mathematical form is concerned, the model leads to the correct result for prothetic continua; however, the exponent B appears to be from one to two orders of magnitude larger than that obtained by direct methods. Stevens [1957] reports $B = 0.3$ for loudness when intensity is measured in energy units.   In a study of loudness discrimination of white noise (the results are fairly similar to those for pure tones) Miller [1947] employed a technique in which the base stimulus was always present and periodically an increment of energy was added.   He reports that for the middle and high intensities the Weber fraction (similar to $c(\pi)$ above) corresponding to 50 per cent correct reports is 0.099 when intensity is measured in energy units.   These data are not of the form needed for this model, since Miller did not use a forced choice technique—a failure to report an increment added is really an indifference report.   If we suppose that in a forced choice situation half of these indifference reports would go one way and half the other—this is not strictly true but, as will be shown, it will not affect the qualitative nature of the calculation—then $\pi = 0.75$ and $c(\pi) = 0.099$.   Substituting these in the above formula yields $B = 11.6$.   Even if we took π as small as 0.6, our formula for B would yield 4.3, which is an order of magnitude larger than Stevens' constant for loudness.

The exact meaning of this discrepancy is at the moment uncertain, and further work, much of it empirical, will be needed to understand it.   One suggestion is that it arises because the time intervals between stimulus presentations in the magnitude estimation procedure are different from the intervals in the discrimination experiments—the interval in the former being much longer than in the latter.   Although a study should be done in which the two procedures are made as nearly identical as possible, it is doubtful that this can be the full explanation.   In section 2.C.5 another explanation is suggested.

3. An Alternative Approach[5]

We can approach the psychophysical scaling problem in a slightly different way, making the linear generalization of Weber's law a conse-

---

[5] The idea contained in this section has been amplified more fully since the book was written; see Luce [1959].

quence rather than an assumption for some continua. Suppose we have
a continuum whose physical measure is a ratio scale, e.g., weight or length,
and suppose that axiom 1 holds. It is reasonable to demand that a change
in the physical unit of measurement do no more than change the unit of
measurement of the subjective scale, i.e.,

$$v(kx) = Kv(x).$$

(This condition is not unlike the independence-of-unit condition discussed
in section 1.F.1.) By the results in Luce and Edwards [1958], the solution
to this equation is unique except for multiplication by a positive constant.
It is easy to see that

$$v(x) = A[x + C]^B,$$

where C is measured in the same units as x, is a solution. Reversing the
argument in section 2.B.1, this form, plus the consequence of axiom 1 that

$$P(x, y) = \frac{v(x)}{v(x) + v(y)},$$

implies that the linear generalization of Weber's law must hold.

4. Two Other Scales

Stevens' characterization of metathetic continua is given in the quota-
tion cited on p. 42. Since, in essence, this class includes all continua that
are not prothetic, it is not surprising that it is less unitary and well behaved
than the one that is positively defined. Possibly this comment is no more
than a rephrasing of the observation that "Psychologically speaking, size
is more scalable than sort." (Stevens and Galanter [1957], p. 401.)

Stated more positively, however, the most distinguishing feature at
present of metathetic continua appears to be the subjective uniformity of
discrimination throughout the ranges of the scales. Metathetic jnds
seem to be constant in subjective size, whereas prothetic jnds increase as
one goes up the scale.

The most obvious hypothesis, no matter what the actual physical jnd
function may be, is to suppose that magnitude estimation elicits a close
relative of the v-scale for prothetic continua, whereas the Fechnerian
scale—log v—results from magnitude estimates of metathetic continua.
This, however, seems dreadfully *ad hoc* unless some plausible reason for
the existence of two or more types of scales can be offered. Such a reason
is suggested in the next section, but before that two other alternatives
should be discarded.

It would be nice if magnitude estimation scales and v-scales were always
of the same general form, as they are for prothetic continua, so let us

suppose for the moment that they are. We have two hints about the possible shape of the subjective scale for metathetic continua. First, the apparent success of Fechnerian—equal subjective jnd—analysis for metathetic continua suggests that the scale might be approximately of the form $v(x) = A \log x + B$. If so, let us determine the π-jnd function by considering

$$P(x, y) = \cfrac{1}{1 + \cfrac{A \log y + B}{A \log x + B}}$$

$$= \pi.$$

From this it follows that

$$(1 - \pi) \log x = \pi \log y + \frac{B}{A} (2\pi - 1).$$

Taking exponentials and making a few algebraic manipulations, we find the following expression for the Weber fraction:

$$\frac{x - y}{y} = (ye^{\frac{B}{A}})^{\frac{2\pi - 1}{1 - \pi}} - 1.$$

For $\pi = 0.75$, $(2\pi - 1)/(1 - \pi) = 2$. But discrimination data do not exhibit Weber fractions that rise so rapidly as the square of the stimulus value; hence the logarithmic v-scale hypothesis must be rejected.

The other hint is that, at least for some ranges, discrimination is independent of the stimulus value, i.e.,

$$P(x, y) = \pi \quad \text{if and only if} \quad x - y = c(\pi).$$

By direct substitution we can show that

$$v(x) = Ce^{Dx},$$

where

$$C > 0 \quad \text{and} \quad D = \frac{\log \pi - \log (1 - \pi)}{c(\pi)},$$

solves the resulting functional equation. Note that for reasonable values, say $\pi = 0.75$ and $c(0.75) = 0.05$, D is of the order of 10. Such a rapidly increasing function seems not in accord with what is found by magnitude estimation procedures, hence it appears that the hypothesis that magnitude estimation invariably produces a function of the same form as the v-scale must be rejected. We turn, therefore, to the question of why the v-scale should appear sometimes and the Fechnerian scale at other times.

C. INTERACTION OF CONTINUA

1. Introduction

It is conventional to discuss psychophysical problems as if there were only one physical continuum involved and to suppress all reference to any others that are inevitably exhibited by the stimuli: a tone of given intensity must also have a frequency, a light of certain wavelength must also have an intensity, etc. In any given experiment the stimuli are chosen so that values on all continua except the one under consideration are held constant, and these constants are treated as implicit parameters. If, however, they are not held constant, they must be introduced explicitly as parameters. For example, suppose that there are two continua (such as intensity and frequency) with typical values $x, y, \cdots$ on the one and $\xi, \eta, \cdots$ on the other; then the assumption that Weber's law holds on the former would have to be written

$$P(x, y; \xi) = \pi \quad \text{if and only if} \quad x = [1 + c(\pi, \xi)]y,$$

and the resulting v-scale would be of the form

$$v(x, \xi) = A(\xi)x^{B(\xi)}.$$

Similarly, if stimuli are varied along the second continuum and Weber's law is again assumed to be true, we get a v-scale that may be written

$$v^*(x, \xi) = A^*(x)\xi^{B^*(x)}.$$

At first glance it might appear that $v(x, \xi)$ and $v^*(x, \xi)$ each define a surface over the physical (x, ξ) plane; however, matters are really not quite that simple. Empirically, all that we can determine is the ratio

$$f(x, y; \xi) = v(x, \xi)/v(y, \xi)$$

for each ξ and the ratio

$$f^*(x; \xi, \eta) = v^*(x, \xi)/v^*(x, \eta)$$

for each x. Thus, for each ξ a ratio scale as a function of x is determined, but there is no necessary relation between the unit of the scale corresponding to one ξ and the unit of the scale for a different ξ. So, in fact, no surface is specified because the unit is arbitrary for each ξ separately; rather, there is a continuum of unrelated curves. Similarly, for each x, f^* determines a ratio scale which is a function of ξ, and there is no relation between the scale units corresponding to two different x's.

Since these units are all arbitrary, certain specific choices can be made for them without doing violence to the data from which the ratio scales are determined. This is done as follows. Let (x_0, ξ_0) be a specific point in the physical plane and set

$$v(x_0, \xi_0) = v^*(x_0, \xi_0) = c > 0.$$

Now choose the units of the v-scales so that they coincide with the form of the v^*-scales for $x = x_0$, i.e.,

$$\frac{v(x_0, \xi)}{v(x_0, \xi_0)} = \frac{v^*(x_0, \xi)}{v^*(x_0, \xi_0)} = f^*(x_0; \xi, \xi_0).$$

Rewriting,

$$v(x_0, \xi) = cf^*(x_0; \xi, \xi_0).$$

This choice completely defines the v-surface up to multiplication by a positive constant because

$$v(x, \xi) = \frac{v(x, \xi)}{v(x_0, \xi)} v(x_0, \xi)$$

$$= cf(x, x_0; \xi)f^*(x_0; \xi, \xi_0).$$

In a similar fashion choose the units of the v^*-scales so that they coincide with the form of the v-scale for $\xi = \xi_0$. A similar computation yields

$$v^*(x, \xi) = cf(x, x_0; \xi_0)f^*(x; \xi, \xi_0).$$

Given a choice of the arbitrary constant for the v-surface, the v^*-surface is uniquely specified; furthermore, as is easily seen, the two surfaces coincide along the lines $x = x_0$ and $\xi = \xi_0$. In the remainder of the discussion the symbols v and v^* refer to these two specific surfaces which, together, are unique except for a multiplicative positive constant.

Consider the shapes of these surfaces for, say, intensity and frequency of tones. From the graphs presented by Licklider [1951], we know that the loudness jnd is a decreasing function of frequency (up to a fairly high frequency), and so, if we assume Weber's law as a first approximation, the exponent of the power law is an increasing function of frequency. Furthermore, for any x, v^* is an increasing function of ξ, so along $x = x_0$ we have forced the v-surface to be an increasing function of ξ. Putting these facts together, we see that the v-surface must increase along any radius from the origin that lies in the positive quadrant of the (x, ξ) plane—the surface is like one quarter of a soup bowl.

A perfectly parallel argument holds for the v^*-surface, since the pitch jnd is a decreasing function of intensity. Thus the two surfaces are of the same general form and they coincide along two orthogonal lines. It is therefore not inconceivable that they coincide everywhere. That certainly is the simplest assumption to make—an assumption which might be argued on grounds of nature's economy.[6] *Note:* We cannot reject this assumption by arguing that it means the point (x, ξ) will be called "louder" than (x', ξ'), $x' \neq x$, $\xi' \neq \xi$ with the same probability that it will be said to have higher pitch because the only direct behavioral meaning that can be given to the surfaces is along the two families of orthogonal lines parallel to the x and ξ axes. That is, the surfaces contain no more information than was used to generate them. The only way to reject the assumption that they are identical is by deducing behaviorally false implications from it or by a direct calculation of the surfaces from data. The data now in existence do not seem to be sufficiently good to warrant the detailed calculations that would be needed, so let us simply see where our assumption leads.

We may state it formally:

Assumption. *If v and v^* are the two surfaces described above, then, for all $x, \xi > 0$, $v(x, \xi) = v^*(x, \xi)$.*

2. Form of v(x, ξ)

Assume for the moment that Weber's law holds on both continua. This coupled with the identity of the two surfaces implies

$$A(\xi)x^{B(\xi)} = A^*(x)\xi^{B^*(x)}, \tag{1}$$

where the A's and B's are unknown positive functions to be determined. With no practical loss of generality, suppose that all of these functions are differentiable.

Take the logarithm of equation 1:

$$\log A(\xi) + B(\xi) \log x = \log A^*(x) + B^*(x) \log \xi. \tag{2}$$

Take the partial derivative of equation 2 with respect to ξ:

$$\frac{dA(\xi)/d\xi}{A(\xi)} + \frac{dB(\xi)}{d\xi} \log x = \frac{B^*(x)}{\xi}. \tag{3}$$

Take the partial derivative of equation 3 with respect to x:

$$\frac{dB(\xi)/d\xi}{x} = \frac{dB^*(x)/dx}{\xi},$$

or rewriting,

$$\xi \frac{dB(\xi)}{d\xi} = x \frac{dB^*(x)}{dx}. \tag{4}$$

Since the variables are separated in equation 4, it follows that each of the

---

[6] A better argument for the same assumption can be found in Luce [1959].

terms must equal a constant, say C, so $B(\xi)$ satisfies the simple differential equation

$$\frac{dB(\xi)}{d\xi} = \frac{C}{\xi},$$

whence

$$B(\xi) = C \log \xi + B, \tag{5}$$

where B is a constant. In like manner,

$$B^*(x) = C \log x + B^*. \tag{6}$$

Substituting equations 5 and 6 in equation 1, we see that

$$A(\xi)x^{C\log\xi}x^B = A^*(x)\xi^{C\log x}\xi^{B^*},$$

but, since

$$x^{C\log\xi} = \xi^{C\log x},$$

it follows immediately that

$$A(\xi)/\xi^{B^*} = A^*(x)/x^B. \tag{7}$$

Once again, the separation of the variables means that each term of equation 7 is a constant, say K, and so equation 1 reduces to

$$v(x, \xi) = K\xi^{B^*}x^{B+C\log\xi}.$$
$$= Kx^B\xi^{B^*+C\log x}. \tag{8}$$

Equation 8 suggests why there may be more than one class of scales. We began with perfectly symmetric assumptions about the two continua and were led to equation 8 which, although equally symmetric in the sense that the v-scale can be expressed in two ways that together are symmetric, is not symmetric once a decision is made which way to write it. Presumably, nature would be forced to such a choice, even if there is no a priori way of deciding which; and with no loss of generality we may suppose that it is

$$v(x, \xi) = K\xi^{B^*}x^{B+C\log\xi}.$$

Let us consider several specializations of the constants. Suppose $C = 0$, then v is simply the product of two simple v-scales, i.e., both of the continua are prothetic. Furthermore, there is no interaction between the two continua so far as discrimination is concerned because

$$P(x, y; \xi) = \frac{1}{1 + (y/x)^B}$$

and

$$P(\xi, \eta; x) = \frac{1}{1 + (\eta/\xi)^{B^*}}.$$

Since variations of one continuum usually affect discrimination on the other, we would not expect (according to this argument) ever to find two prothetic continua locked together; however, see the results in the next section when Weber's law is weakened.

Next suppose $B^* = 0$, then

$$v(x, \xi) = x^{B+C\log \xi}.$$

With ξ held constant, we find the power law for x, but, with x held constant, the v-scale is written as a constant raised to a power, namely, the Fechnerian scale value. This certainly suggests that there is an inherent difference between the two scales, and possibly this is the formal counterpart of the difference discussed by Stevens. Observe that in this case discrimination on one continuum is not independent of the value selected for the other; moreover, the dependence of the jnd function for one continuum as a function of values on the other continuum can be calculated. A numerical illustration is given below.

Observe that if neither B^* nor C equals 0, then, although the x-continuum is still prothetic, the form of the ξ-continuum is much more complicated: in part it is like a prothetic continuum and in part it is like a pure metathetic continuum. This mathematical possibility suggests that it may be necessary to subdivide the nonprothetic continua further into several distinct classes. Such a logical possibility seems to be supported by the difficulty experimentalists have had in trying to ascribe uniform properties to the metathetic scales as a group.

One final observation: at least one of the continua must be prothetic if this argument is correct.

3. Generalizations

Such an analysis may explain why there are several classes of continua when Weber's law holds, but it says nothing for other jnd functions. As it stands, therefore, it is severely limited and can only be said to suggest an approach to the general problem. Unfortunately, severer mathematical difficulties are encountered in other cases. For example, the linear generalization of Weber's law leads to the functional equation

$$v(x, \xi) = A(\xi)[x + C(\xi)]^{B(\xi)}$$
$$= A^*(x)[\xi + C^*(x)]^{B^*(x)},$$

where the A's and the B's must be positive functions, since v is a positive ratio scale that increases with the physical variable. By direct substitution we can easily see that

$$v(x, \xi) = (ax + b)^{B+C\log(c\xi+d)}(c\xi + d)^{B^*}$$

and

$$v(x, \xi) = (ax + b\xi + cx\xi + d)^B,$$

where a, b, c, d, B, B^*, and C are numerical constants, are both solutions to the equation. I have been unable to show that they are the only solutions (the analogue of the method used for Weber's law does not push through so easily). Nonetheless, this slight generalization admits at least one inherently new possibility (the second solution) which can be interpreted as two prothetic continua that interact.

For other jnd functions, e.g., the linear generalization of Weber's law on one continuum and jnds that are independent of the stimulus value on the other, one will apparently have to attack the problem anew, using whatever techniques seem to work to tease out the possible solutions.

4. A Numerical Example

Let us, for the sake of the argument, suppose that Weber's law holds for both the intensity and frequency continua of tones, and from this let us calculate the intensity (x-continuum) jnd as a function of frequency. Equation 8 can be written

$$v(x, \xi) = K\xi^{B^*}x^{C\log(\xi/R)}.$$

If π is a fixed probability cutoff and the frequency is ξ, then x is one π-jnd above y when

$$P(x, y; \xi) = \pi$$

$$= \frac{1}{1 + \dfrac{v(y, \xi)}{v(x, \xi)}}$$

$$= \frac{1}{1 + (y/x)^{C\log(\xi/R)}}.$$

We shall hold y fixed and determine the ratio x/y as ξ is varied; call this ratio $\gamma(\xi)$. Solving the above equation, we get

$$\log \gamma(\xi) = \frac{\log \pi/(1 - \pi)}{C \log (\xi/R)},$$

so

$$\frac{\log \gamma(\xi)}{\log \gamma(\eta)} = \frac{\log (\eta/R)}{\log (\xi/R)}.$$

For frequency, the threshold R is in the neighborhood of 10 cps, so for convenience we set $R = 10$. Now, if the value of $\gamma(\eta)$ for one frequency is known, then all of the other values of γ are determined. For example, reading the curves by eye on p. 999 of Licklider [1951] it appears that for an intensity 70 db above a reference level the ratio x/y is 0.35 db for $\eta = 1000$ cps. For other choices of frequency, the predicted and observed values of $\gamma(\xi)$ are presented in Table 2. It is clear from the drawing in

TABLE 2. Predicted and Observed $\gamma(\xi)$ as a Function of ξ for an Intensity 70 db above a Standard. $\gamma(1000)$ Was Chosen to Have the Observed Value of 0.35 db

$\gamma(\xi)$ in db

ξ in cps	Predicted	Observed
20	2.33	—
50	1.00	1.0
100	0.70	0.5
500	0.41	0.4
5,000	0.26	0.3
10,000	0.23	0.3
15,000	0.22	0.3

the Licklider article that for all levels of intensity $\gamma(\xi)$ decreases with increasing ξ up to a point and then begins to increase. It is equally clear that our equations do not exhibit this phenomenon. Whether this merely reflects the crudeness of the Weber law approximation to the jnd function, whether it is not a real phenomenon as some have charged, but an artifact of Riesz's procedure, or whether the analysis we have given contains an inherent error [most likely the assumption that $v(x, \xi) = v^*(x, \xi)$], it is not at present known.

5. The Power Law Exponent

As pointed out in section 2.B, the exponent of the power law is at least one order of magnitude smaller when determined from magnitude estimation data than when calculated from discrimination data. The preceding analysis of the several classes of scales suggests a possible reason for this. Suppose that $B^* = 0$ in equation 8; then we can write it as

$$v(x, \xi) = x^{C \log(\xi/R)}$$
$$= x^{\alpha[(C/\alpha)\log(\xi/R)]},$$

where α is some constant. Now, suppose that these scales are stored separately as x^{α} and $(C/\alpha) \log (\xi/R)$ and that in magnitude estimation these are the functions elicited. Although presently speculative, this idea is not untestable, since it implies that the numbers obtained from discrimination data, from magnitude estimation of the x-continuum, and from magnitude estimation of the ξ-continuum are not independent.

Specifically, suppose that x is tone intensity and ξ is tone frequency; then from the calculation in section 2.B we know that $C \log \xi/R$ is about 12 for, say, $\xi = 1000$. Using logarithms to the base 10, it follows that $C = \frac{12}{2} = 6$. Thus for every frequency decade we would expect the subject to use a numerical range of $6/\alpha$, so for the whole frequency range of 10 to 10,000 cps the range would be $18/\alpha$. For a subject with an intensity exponent of 0.3, as reported by Stevens, the range of numbers used in magnitude estimation of frequency would be predicted to be $18/0.3$, or about 60. Over a population of subjects we also predict an inverse correlation between the intensity exponent and the range of numerical values assigned to frequency.

D. DISCRIMINAL PROCESSES

1. Introduction

Thurstone [1927a,b] introduced the concept of a "discriminal process" both as a possible explanation of imperfect discrimination and as a means of extending psychophysical analysis to stimuli not obviously lying on a single physical continuum. As this notion has been a key to much psychometric work since then, it seems appropriate to examine some of the simpler relations between that notion and the present theory.

In its simplest form the idea is to assume that stimuli have numerical scale values u and to attach a density function $f_{u(x)}(t)$ to each numerical stimulus value $u(x)$. This function is interpreted as the probability density that the subject thought a stimulus with value t was presented when x having value $u(x)$ was actually administered. Let x and y denote two different sound energies; then the model postulates that an observation is drawn from the distribution $f_{u(x)}(t)$ and another from $f_{u(y)}(t)$, and whichever is the larger determines which stimulus the subject calls louder. Formally, let

$$F_{u(x)}(t) = \int_{-\infty}^{t} f_{u(x)}(\tau)\, d\tau;$$

then, if the observations are independent, it is assumed that

$$P(x, y) = \int_{-\infty}^{\infty} f_{u(x)}(t) F_{u(y)}(t)\, dt.$$

If there is a correlation between the drawings for x and for y, we are obliged to work with the joint density function.

For the most part the following tack has been taken. The numerical scale u over the set U of stimuli is assumed to be such that the densities induced upon this scale are normal. The arguments for this definition of a scale are not substantive; rather, they seem to stem from the ubiquitousness of the normal distribution in "error" problems and from its many convenient properties. The usefulness of the assumption or the possibility that it can be subjected to certain indirect empirical tests are not being questioned, but only its a priori plausibility and its role as a fundamental psychological postulate. Thurstone singled out five cases for special attention, of which case V has been most widely used. This case is characterized by the assumptions that the variances of the several distributions are all the same (an assumption very similar to Fechner's equal jnds) and that the correlations between every pair of distributions is the same (which can be taken to be 0, since there is no way to distinguish what the constant value is). It can then be shown that the relation between the discrimination probabilities and the scale u is

$$P(x, y) = \frac{1}{\sqrt{2\pi}} \int_{-\infty}^{\frac{u(x)-u(y)}{\sigma}} \exp \frac{-t^2}{2} \, dt,$$

where σ is the unknown standard deviation.

2. Relation of Axiom 1 to Thurstone's Case V

It is immediately clear that this function is logically distinct from the logistic function

$$P(x, y) = \frac{1}{1 + \exp\{-k[u(x) - u(y)]\}},$$

for otherwise the integral of the normal could be expressed in terms of elementary functions, which is well known to be false. However, for most practical purposes they are the same. This we may show by a calculation.

From the corollary to theorem 2 we know that axiom 1 implies that

$$P(x, z) = \frac{P(x, y)P(y, z)}{P(x, y)P(y, z) + P(z, y)P(y, x)},$$

so for various pairs $P(x, y)$ and $P(y, z)$ we may table the predicted values of $P(x, z)$; similarly, in Thurstone's case V, knowing $P(x, y)$ allows us to compute $[u(x) - u(y)]/\sigma$ and knowing $P(y, z)$ gives us $[u(y) - u(z)]/\sigma$. Since

$$\frac{u(x) - u(z)}{\sigma} = \frac{u(x) - u(y)}{\sigma} + \frac{u(y) - u(z)}{\sigma},$$

we can, therefore, calculate $P(x, z)$. The results are shown in Table 3, and the differences are seen to be small—the largest is less than two parts in a hundred.

TABLE 3. Comparison of Predicted P(x, z) from Known P(x, y) and P(y, z) Using Axiom 1 and Thurstone's Case V.

	$P(y, z)$						$P(y, z)$			
	0.6	0.7	0.8	0.9			0.6	0.7	0.8	0.9
$P(x, y)$ 0.6	0.692	0.778	0.857	0.931		$P(x, y)$ 0.6	0.695	0.782	0.864	0.938
0.7		0.845	0.903	0.954		0.7		0.853	0.915	0.965
0.8			0.941	0.973		0.8			0.954	0.983
0.9				0.988		0.9				0.995

$P(x, z)$ from axiom 1 $P(x, z)$ from Thurstone's case V

Thus the two assumptions are extremely similar for all practical purposes, although they are logically distinct, and so the choice between them must rest upon other considerations, such as convenience and depth and range of consequences. Among other things, the ability of the present theory to deal with zero and one probabilities explicitly seems a point in its favor.

It should be emphasized that no inconsistency has been established for pairwise discriminations between the logistic resulting from axiom 1 and a variety of other Thurstone models. Keeping normality, the assumptions of constant variances and constant correlations can be abandoned, and, furthermore, the normality assumption can be relaxed. No results are known concerning the relation between the two models in these cases.

3. A Generalization to Three or More Alternatives

If Thurstone's concept of a discriminal process underlying imperfect discrimination corresponds to any reality, it would appear only reasonable that it should extend to more than two alternatives. Specifically, if arbitrary densities are assumed (subject only to the condition that the integrals written below are defined), and if the correlation is zero (independence), then

$$P_T(x) = \int_{-\infty}^{\infty} f_{u(x)}(t) \prod_{y \in T - \{x\}} F_{u(y)}(t) \, dt. \tag{9}$$

Given the way this equation is written, $P_T(x)$ must be interpreted as the probability that x is judged the largest (or loudest or most superior in some way) alternative in T. Equally well, the subject could be asked to choose the smallest, and there would be some probability $P_T^*(x)$ that x is so judged. In that event Thurstone's model would be

$$P_T^*(x) = \int_{-\infty}^{\infty} f_{u(x)}(t) \prod_{y \in T - \{x\}} [1 - F_{u(y)}(t)] \, dt. \tag{10}$$

Since axiom 1 was in no way restricted to choices based upon one criterion (such as largest) rather than another (such as smallest), it seems plausible to suppose that it holds for P^* as well as for P. The connection between these two sets of probabilities is, of course, established via the pairwise case for which it is reasonable to suppose that $P^*(x, y) = P(y, x)$.

We now show that if a zero correlation version of Thurstone's model is extended in the foregoing manner to sets of three elements then no density function is consistent with the assumption that P and P^* both satisfy axiom 1 for three-element sets.

Theorem 7. *Let P and P^* be defined for $T = \{x, y, z\}$ and its subsets, where $T \subset U$. Suppose that*

(i) $P(r, s) \neq 0, 1$ for $r, s \in T$,
(ii) $P(x, y) + P(x, z) \neq 1$,
(iii) P and P^* *both satisfy axiom 1,*
(iv) $P^*(x, y) = P(y, x)$,

then there do not exist a scale u on U and density functions $f_{u(r)}(t)$, $r \in T$ and t real, such that equations 9 and 10 hold for T.

PROOF. Suppose the theorem is false, then by equations 9 and 10

$$
\begin{aligned}
P_T(x) - P_T^*(x) &= \int_{-\infty}^{\infty} f_{u(x)}(t) \{F_{u(y)}(t) F_{u(z)}(t) \\
&\qquad\qquad - [1 - F_{u(y)}(t)][1 - F_{u(z)}(t)]\} \, dt \\
&= \int_{-\infty}^{\infty} f_{u(x)}(t) [F_{u(y)}(t) + F_{u(z)}(t) - 1] \, dt \\
&= P(x, y) + P(x, z) - 1.
\end{aligned}
$$

However, by theorem 1 and hypothesis iv,

$$P_T(x) - P_T^*(x)$$

$$
= \cfrac{1}{1 + \cfrac{P(y, x)}{P(x, y)} + \cfrac{P(z, x)}{P(x, z)}} - \cfrac{1}{1 + \cfrac{P^*(y, x)}{P^*(x, y)} + \cfrac{P^*(z, x)}{P^*(x, z)}}
$$

$$
= \cfrac{1}{1 + \cfrac{1 - P(x, y)}{P(x, y)} + \cfrac{1 - P(x, z)}{P(x, z)}} - \cfrac{1}{1 + \cfrac{P(x, y)}{1 - P(x, y)} + \cfrac{P(x, z)}{1 - P(x, z)}}
$$

$$
= [P(x, y) + P(x, z) - 1]
$$
$$
\left\{ \frac{P(x, y) + P(x, z) - 2P(x, y)P(x, z)}{[P(x, y) + P(x, z) - P(x, y)P(x, z)][1 - P(x, y)P(x, z)]} \right\}.
$$

By hypothesis ii, $P(x, y) + P(x, z) - 1 \neq 0$, so for these two expressions to be equal it is necessary that the term in braces be 1. Simplifying,

$$P(x, y)P(y, x)P(x, z)P(z, x) = 0,$$

which contradicts hypothesis i.

It should be emphasized that this contradiction is obtained only under the assumption of statistically independent discriminal processes, an assumption that many doubt is true. No results are known when there are dependencies, but it is hard not to believe that with both dependencies and arbitrary density functions one could fit nearly any other theory.

E. SIGNAL DETECTABILITY THEORY

1. Introduction

If, let us say, an acoustic tone of known intensity and frequency is presented in a background of noise of known characteristics, what is the probability that a person will detect its presence? And in what manner, if at all, does this probability vary with the reward and information parameters that are under the experimenter's control? Specifically, does a priori knowledge of the probability of a signal's occurrence affect its probability of detection and does differential treatment of the subject's errors alter it? These, roughly, are the types of problems that have been treated recently in signal detectability theory. The main published references to this work are Tanner and Swets [1954a,b], Tanner and Norman [1954], and Swets and Birdsall [1956]. In addition, there are a number of technical reports by Tanner and others issued by the Engineering Research Institute, The University of Michigan, Ann Arbor.

The problem is, of course, old—about as old as psychophysics itself. Traditionally, it has been known as the threshold problem, but that term severely pre-judges the solution by implying that a threshold does in fact exist and that the only task is to measure it. The thesis of the signal detectability school is that thresholds do not exist in the classic sense, and, by varying the payoffs, they have demonstrated that a subject's probability of detection can be manipulated over a broad range. Instead of the threshold model, they have postulated that people behave to some degree as if they were statisticians attempting to maximize their expected payoffs by selecting certain decision parameters under their control and applying the resulting criterion to the fallible data that result from their observations of the signal.

The signal detectability model divides nicely into two quite distinct parts. The first describes the information that is "internally" available to the subject as a result of the stimulus situation. On the basis of this information he must reach his decision. The second describes his decision-making characteristics. He is thought of as a decision maker of the statistical variety who must, in the light of prior information and payoffs, select a decision criterion from a family of possibilities and apply it to the information arising from the first model. Together, the two models determine his probability of detecting the signal. In all of their work they have employed a Thurstonian discriminal process type model for part one, and in much of it they have assumed that the subject maximizes expected monetary return as the decision model. In addition, other decision criteria have been discussed and some of the mathematics worked out. There is some indication that by experimental manipulations subjects can be induced to use different criteria.

Given the results from the preceding section, it is not surprising that a closely parallel model can be worked out in terms of axiom 1, and, as usual, it is simpler and more readily generalized than the corresponding Thurstone model.

2. Yes-No Experiments

Most of the signal detectability work has concentrated on the analysis of the so-called Yes-No experimental paradigm. Here a subject knows that on any trial he may be confronted by noise alone or by signal plus noise and he is to report which he believes it is. In rough outline, the Thurstonian model used by the signal detection theorists postulates an underlying decision continuum, an observation made by the subject being assumed to reduce to a single point on this continuum. The distribution of observations resulting from noise alone is assumed to be normal, with some unknown mean and variance. This distribution is assumed to be displaced to the right, and possibly the variance altered, when a signal is added to the noise. The amount of displacement is of

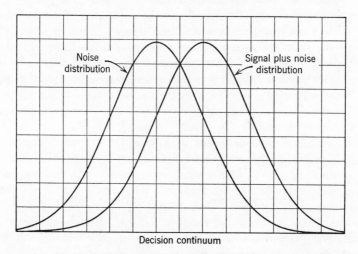

Decision continuum

Figure 3. Distribution of observations on the decision continuum postulated in the signal detectability model of the Yes-No experiment.

course a function of the signal strength. The subject's problem is, given an observation, to decide which of the two distributions is more likely to have fathered it. Rather clearly, this reduces to selecting a cutoff point on the continuum such that if his observation exceeds the cutoff he asserts "Yes, the signal is there," and if it is less he announces "No, it is not."

The decision-making model is concerned with optimal choices of the cutoff point in the light of the payoffs and prior information, but let us postpone discussion of that.

It will be observed that no matter where he sets his cutoff there will, in general, be errors of both types: sometimes he will say a signal is there when there is none and other times that there is none when in fact it is there. The relation between these two probabilities as the cutoff is varied tells much about the two distributions, assuming that they exist. It has become customary to plot not that relationship but rather a closely related one: the probability of an affirmative answer when the signal is present as a function of the same probability when there is no signal. For each displacement between the distributions, i.e., signal strength, a different curve is obtained. Some of these curves, which are known as Receiver Operating Characteristics (or R.O.C. curves), are shown as the dotted lines in Figure 4. The parameter d' is a normalized measure of the separation between the two distributions; it is, of course, not an observable, but rather must be inferred from the behavioral data under the assumption that the model is true. In addition, a theory has been devised relating d' to physical properties of the noise and the signal.

The axiom 1 analysis of this experiment follows almost immediately from the statement of the situation and the analysis carried out in section 1.F. There are two stimulus conditions, either signal and noise (SN) or noise alone (N), and two response categories, either affirm (A) or not affirm ($\sim A$). Using the same assumptions as in section 1.F and fixing the effect of the noise alone as 1, we immediately write down the v-scale values as

$$\begin{array}{cc} & \begin{array}{cc} A & \sim A \end{array} \\ \begin{array}{c} SN \\ N \end{array} & \left[\begin{array}{cc} \alpha_1 v_1 & \alpha_2 v_2 \\ v_1 & v_2 \end{array}\right], \end{array}$$

which can be reduced to

$$\begin{array}{cc} & \begin{array}{cc} A & \sim A \end{array} \\ \begin{array}{c} SN \\ N \end{array} & \left[\begin{array}{cc} \alpha & v \\ 1 & v \end{array}\right] = \left[\begin{array}{cc} \alpha & 1 \\ 1 & 1 \end{array}\right]\left[\begin{array}{cc} 1 & 0 \\ 0 & v \end{array}\right], \end{array}$$

where $v = v_2/v_1$ and $\alpha = \alpha_1/\alpha_2$.

If P_{ij} denotes the probability associated with the ith row and the jth column, then

$$P_{11} = \frac{\alpha}{\alpha + v} \quad \text{and} \quad P_{21} = \frac{1}{1 + v} \cdot$$

Eliminating v, we find

$$P_{11} = \frac{\alpha P_{21}}{(\alpha - 1)P_{21} + 1}$$

as the equation of the R.O.C. curve.   These are plotted as the solid lines in Figure 4.

Although the R.O.C. curves from the two models are practically indistinguishable, there is a significant difference of interpretation. In the signal detectability model the subject selects a cutoff point along a decision axis, whereas in the axiom 1 model he selects a response bias.

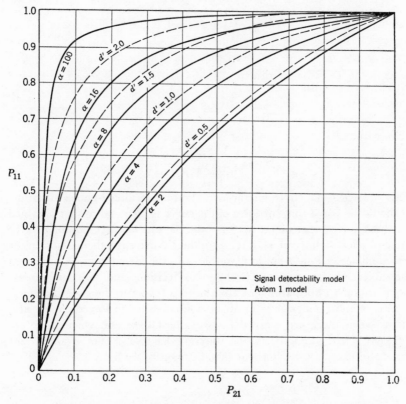

Figure 4.   Receiver operating characteristics for signal detectability and axiom 1 models of the Yes-No experiment. P_{11} denotes the probability of an affirmative response when the signal is present in the noise, and P_{21}, the probability of an affirmative response when only noise is present.

The latter model and its interpretation seem to be more readily generalized to more complex experiments.

3. Forced-Choice Experiments

A closely related experimental procedure is to present the subject with two successive time intervals, one or the other of which contains the signal as well as noise and the other, noise alone. The subject is to assert which interval contains the signal. This is exactly the two-stimulus version of the model discussed in section 1.F.:

$$\begin{array}{cc} & \begin{array}{cc} 1 & 2 \end{array} \\ \begin{array}{c} SN, N \\ N, SN \end{array} & \left[\begin{array}{cc} \alpha v_1 & v_2 \\ v_1 & \alpha v_2 \end{array}\right] \end{array}$$

which reduces to

$$\begin{array}{cc} & \begin{array}{cc} 1 & 2 \end{array} \\ \begin{array}{c} SN, N \\ N, SN \end{array} & \left[\begin{array}{cc} \alpha & v \\ 1 & \alpha v \end{array}\right], \end{array}$$

where $v = v_2/v_1$.

As in the Yes-No experiment,

$$P_{11} = \frac{\alpha}{\alpha + v} \quad \text{and} \quad P_{21} = \frac{1}{1 + \alpha v}.$$

Eliminating v,

$$P_{11} = \frac{\alpha^2 P_{21}}{(\alpha^2 - 1)P_{21} + 1}.$$

This is the R.O.C. curve for the two-alternative, forced-choice situation. It should be noted that the form of the curve is identical to that obtained for the Yes-No experiment; however the parameter corresponding to the same physical signal differs: if it is α in the Yes-No case, then it is α^2 in the forced choice. This is not implausible. In the forced-choice experiment the subject makes, in effect, two Yes-No decisions and so has in a sense twice as much information entering into his report to the experimenter.

This analysis generalizes in an obvious manner to forced-choice situations when there are more than two alternatives and when there are different signal strengths in the different locations. For example, for three alternatives with different signal strengths, we have

$$\begin{array}{cc} & \begin{array}{ccc} 1 & \quad 2 & \quad 3 \end{array} \\ \begin{array}{c} SN, N, N \\ N, SN, N \\ N, N, SN \end{array} & \left[\begin{array}{ccc} \alpha v_1 & v_2 & v_3 \\ v_1 & \beta v_2 & v_3 \\ v_1 & v_2 & \gamma v_3 \end{array}\right]. \end{array}$$

The signal detectability analysis of these more general situations is a good deal more complicated and, to date, has included the unlikely assumption that there is no response bias. They will not be developed here; see Swets and Birdsall [1956].

4. Expected-Value Model

As has been indicated, the signal-detectability theorists next postulate that the subject chooses his point on the appropriate R.O.C. curve by applying some decision criterion. Several are possible, but one of the easiest to work out is an expected-value model.[7] Consider the Yes-No experiment and suppose that the subject knows that the probability of a signal occurring is P and that he will be paid off or fined according to the following payoff matrix:

$$
\begin{array}{cc}
& A \quad \sim A \\
\begin{array}{c} SN \\ N \end{array} & \begin{bmatrix} a & b \\ c & d \end{bmatrix}.
\end{array}
$$

The entries are usually interpreted to be sums of money, but they had better really be some subjective measure of money—i.e., utility—if trivial rejections of the model are to be avoided. The expected value for the axiom 1 model is then

$$
E(V) = P[aP_{11} + bP_{12}] + (1 - P)[cP_{21} + dP_{22}]
$$

$$
= P\left[\frac{a\alpha + bv}{\alpha + v}\right] + (1 - P)\left[\frac{c + dv}{1 + v}\right].
$$

The optimizing criterion states that the subject attempts to maximize the expected value by his choice of the only variable under his control, namely, the response bias v. In the usual signal-detectability model he is assumed to do the same thing through his choice of the cutoff point. Assuming this is what he does, we set the derivative of $E(V)$ equal to 0:

$$
\frac{dE(V)}{dv} = P\left[\frac{(\alpha + v)b - (a\alpha + bv)}{(\alpha + v)^2}\right] + (1 - P)\left[\frac{(1 + v)d - (c + dv)}{(1 + v)^2}\right]
$$

$$
= 0,
$$

so,

$$
\alpha\left(\frac{1 + v}{\alpha + v}\right)^2 = B,
$$

[7] As will become clear in Chapter 3, I have little faith in the descriptive accuracy of the expected-value model; it is included here only as an illustration of the type of analysis used.

where

$$B = \left(\frac{1 - P}{P}\right)\left(\frac{d - c}{a - b}\right).$$

Solving for v, we obtain

$$v = \frac{\sqrt{\alpha B} - 1}{1 - \sqrt{B/\alpha}}.$$

If this is now substituted into the expressions for P_{11} and P_{21}, we obtain a parametric expression for the optimal curves:

$$P_{11} = \frac{\alpha - \sqrt{\alpha B}}{\alpha - 1}$$

$$P_{21} = \frac{\sqrt{\alpha/B} - 1}{\alpha - 1}.$$

The curves obtained by holding B fixed at different values and varying α are shown in Figure 5. It should be noted that so long as the payoffs and the probability P are fixed, B is a constant. Therefore, by varying the signal intensity, the optimizing assumption can be tested without actually supposing that the expected monetary return is being optimized—both the payoffs and the probability P can be interpreted as subjective measures.

The following equalities that hold along the optimal curves should be noted:

$$\frac{dP_{11}}{dP_{21}} = \frac{dP_{11}/dv}{dP_{21}/dv}$$

$$= \alpha \left(\frac{1 + v}{\alpha + v}\right)^2$$

$$= B$$

$$= \frac{1}{\alpha} \left(\frac{P_{11}}{P_{21}}\right)^2.$$

The forced-choice optimal v is determined similarly; it is

$$v = \frac{\alpha \sqrt{B} - 1}{\alpha - \sqrt{B}}.$$

5. Recognition Experiments and Maximum Amounts of Information Transmitted

Recognition, or absolute identification, experiments yield estimates of the probability that stimulus i is confused with stimulus j; such data tables are commonly called confusion matrices. In recent years information theorists have noted that these data seem to indicate that a subject is able to transmit only about three bits of information, no matter how much information is contained in the stimulus presentation (Miller, 1956). Indeed, these results, indicating as they do an information-handling capacity for human subjects, have been regarded as one of the major substantive contributions of information theory to psychology. The

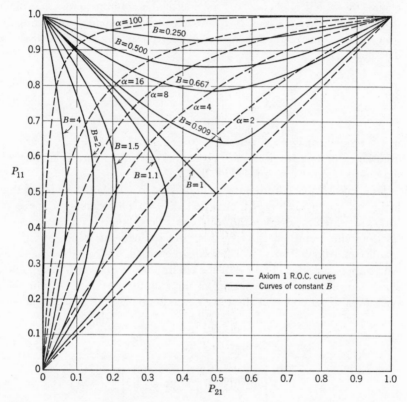

Figure 5. Curves of maximum expected value in Yes-No experiment as a function of signal strength, with payoffs and signal probability fixed.

purpose of this section is to describe a simple model for at least some recognition experiments which leads to a plausible explanation of the maximum information transmission results.

The simplest recognition experiment involves the presentation of either one of two stimuli, S_1 or S_2, on each trial. The subject undertakes to identify which was presented, and he reports his belief by using one of two possible responses, R_1 or R_2, the former if he thinks the stimulus was

S_1 and the latter if it was S_2. For example, the stimuli could be pure tones of the same intensity but different frequencies in a background of noise, in which case the subject would be required to say on each trial whether the higher or the lower frequency was presented.

The model parallels that used for the detection experiments. A two-by-two matrix of scale values, having response biases 1 and v in the two columns and signal parameters in the rows is set up. As before, we may choose the signal effect to be 1 in one of the columns and some other value in the other column, but now it will be convenient to locate the 1 in the opposite position from that employed in the detection analysis. The matrix is

$$
\begin{array}{cc}
& \begin{array}{cc} R_1 & R_2 \end{array} \\
\begin{array}{c} S_1 \\ S_2 \end{array} &
\left[\begin{array}{cc} 1 & \rho_{12}v \\ \rho_{21} & v \end{array} \right],
\end{array}
$$

where the parameters ρ_{ij} lie between 0 and 1 and are interpreted as confusion parameters in the sense that they give the relative loading on response j when stimulus i is presented.

The generalization from 2 to n stimuli is clear. It should be noted that there are $n(n-1) + n - 1 = (n+1)(n-1)$ parameters in the general case, which means that the matrix of scale values is no more economical than the confusion matrix itself, and so, without some simplifying assumptions, further analysis is likely to be messy. We shall suppose, as a first approximation, that all of the confusion parameters are the same, which is to say that, pairwise, all of the stimuli are equally confusable. We shall also suppose that there are no response biases. Thus, the model is

$$
\begin{array}{c}
\begin{array}{ccccc} R_1 & R_2 & R_3 & \dots & R_n \end{array} \\
\begin{array}{c} S_1 \\ S_2 \\ S_3 \\ \\ \\ \\ S_n \end{array}
\left[\begin{array}{ccccc}
1 & \rho & \rho & \dots & \rho \\
\rho & 1 & \rho & \dots & \rho \\
\rho & \rho & 1 & \dots & \rho \\
\cdot & \cdot & \cdot & \cdot & \cdot \\
\cdot & \cdot & \cdot & \cdot & \cdot \\
\cdot & \cdot & \cdot & \cdot & \cdot \\
\rho & \rho & \rho & \dots & 1
\end{array} \right].
\end{array}
$$

It is clear that the first assumption, which is the important one, could be approximately correct for a set of carefully chosen words but that it is likely to be grossly wrong for stimuli, such as tones, that lie on a continuum.

If the stimuli are presented equally often, then by the symmetry of the model we see that the response categories will be used equally often. With this in mind, we compute the amount of information transmitted by the subject:

$$T = H(y) - H_x(y)$$

$$= - \sum_{j=1}^{n} p(j) \log_2 p(j) + \sum_{i=1}^{n} \sum_{j=1}^{n} p(i)(p\,j|i) \log_2 p(j|i),$$

where $p(i)$ is the probability that stimulus i is presented, which by assumption is $1/n$, $p(j)$ is the probability of response j occurring, which by the preceding remark is $1/n$, and $p(j|i)$ is the conditional probability of response j given stimulus i. From the model, we see that

$$p(j|i) = \begin{cases} 1/[1 + (n-1)\rho], & \text{if } j = i \\ \rho/[1 + (n-1)\rho], & \text{if } j \neq i. \end{cases}$$

Substituting,

$$T = \log_2 n + \left[\frac{1}{1 + (n-1)\rho} \right] \log_2 \left[\frac{1}{1 + (n-1)\rho} \right]$$

$$+ \left[\frac{(n-1)\rho}{1 + (n-1)\rho} \right] \log_2 \left[\frac{\rho}{1 + (n-1)\rho} \right]$$

$$= \log_2 \left[\frac{n}{1 + (n-1)\rho} \right] + \left[\frac{(n-1)}{1 + (n-1)\rho} \right] \log_2 \rho.$$

In Figure 6 T is plotted as a function of $\log_2 n$ (the number of bits in the stimulus presentation) for several values of ρ. The values of ρ used are such that the pairwise confusions vary from 0.8 to 9 per cent.

With ρ fixed, the location of the maximum is obtained by setting the derivative of T with respect to n equal to 0. The result is

$$n = \frac{(1-\rho)^2}{\rho} \frac{1}{-\log_e \rho - (1-\rho)}.$$

The curve of the maximum is shown as the dotted line in Figure 6. Note that it is approximately a straight line with slope 1. This can be proved rigorously for large n, but it is also apparently true for rather small n.

The qualitative nature of the curves corresponds to the observations discussed by Miller (1956). A maximum is attained in the range of three to five bits, its value ranges from 1.5 to 3.5 bits, the location of the maximum and its value are correlated, and the amount of information transmitted diminishes following the maximum. On the other hand, the exact curves obtained do not correspond at all well with the data. Whether this means that our explanation is wrong in principle or whether it results from the erroneous approximation that all confusion parameters are equal is not known. Certainly, the approximation is not very satisfactory for the stimuli of the experiments discussed by Miller. This means that we are attempting to use an average confusion parameter

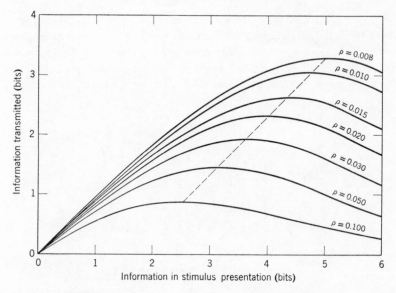

Figure 6. Information transmitted versus information presented for several values of the confusion parameter (see text for explanation of the model). The dotted line indicates the location of the maximum points.

for the true values, and it is well known that this can only increase the apparent values of the information measures. So $H_x(y)$ will be larger in the model than it should be, which means that T will be smaller than it should be. Thus it appears that a more nearly correct model would rotate all of the curves toward the $45°$ line, which is exactly what is needed to handle the data.

F. RANK ORDERINGS

Sometimes subjects are required to rank-order a set of alternatives instead of simply selecting the element that is distinguished in some manner (e.g., the best, or smallest, or loudest, etc.).   Often this is done to ensure that their reports form a weak ordering of the alternatives, for, as pointed out in sections 1.A.1 and 1.D.2, data on choices from all pairs of stimuli do not generally form a transitive relation.   Rankings are also used to obtain indirect data on repeated presentations of a single pair of alternatives without, in fact, presenting the isolated pair a number of times; these data are then used to estimate the pairwise probability of choice.   A possible model for ranking data is presented and results pertaining to each of these uses are proved.

1. Direction of Ranking

The model of ranking behavior to be proposed is, in spirit, closely related to axiom 1; however, it is logically independent of it.   Let $P_T(x)$ denote the probability that x is judged to be the superior element in T according to some specified criterion.   If, for example, $T = \{x, y, z\}$, then let us assume that the probability of ranking T in the order $x > y > z$ (according to this criterion) is given by

$$R(x > y > z) = P_T(x)P(y, z).$$

That is to say, we assume that the subject ranks T by deciding first which alternative is superior according to the criterion and, then, of the two remaining alternatives, deciding which of these is the superior.

An alternative way he could rank T is to decide which alternative is inferior according to the criterion, which is next inferior, and so on.   If we let $P_T^*(x)$ denote the probability that x is judged inferior in T according to the criterion, we have for the probability of the ranking $x > y > z$

$$R^*(x > y > z) = P_T^*(z)P^*(y, x).$$

If we are willing to assume that both P and P^* satisfy axiom 1 (as in section 2.D), then they are related to one another by theorem 1 and by the plausible assumption that $P^*(x, y) = P(y, x)$.   Thus we might anticipate that $R(x > y > z) = R^*(x > y > z)$; unfortunately, this is not generally so.

Theorem 8. *Let P and P^* be defined for $T = \{x, y, z\}$ and its subsets. Suppose that they both satisfy axiom 1, that all pairwise discriminations are imperfect, and that $P^*(x, y) = P(y, x)$. A necessary and sufficient condition for*

$$P_T(x)P(y, z) = P_T^*(z)P(x, y),$$

is that $P(x, y) = P(y, z)$.

PROOF. By theorem 1, the condition is equivalent to

$$\frac{P(y, z)}{1 + \dfrac{1 - P(x, y)}{P(x, y)} + \dfrac{1 - P(x, z)}{P(x, z)}} = \frac{P(x, y)}{1 + \dfrac{1 - P^*(z, x)}{P^*(z, x)} + \dfrac{1 - P^*(z, y)}{P^*(z, y)}}$$

$$= \frac{P(x, y)}{1 + \dfrac{1 - P(x, z)}{P(x, z)} + \dfrac{1 - P(y, z)}{P(y, z)}}$$

A few simple algebraic manipulations yield the result.

The gist of the theorem is that in general it matters whether the subject ranks from top to bottom or from bottom to top, since the two probabilities of the ranking are the same only when the middle alternative is "half way in probability" between the two end alternatives. This fact may not be unrelated to the fairly widespread but apparently undocumented impression that most people exhibit a characteristic direction of ordering, usually from the top down.

The empirical consequences of theorem 8 are somewhat obscure; however, it certainly suggests that great caution is needed in obtaining and interpreting rank-order data. Presumably, we want a subject always to rank alternatives in the same direction so as to minimize the variance introduced, but it is difficult to know what mechanism he is actually using. For example, in a long, dull experiment a subject may, for the sake of variety, attempt to rank from best to worst one time, worst to best another, from the middle out to the two ends at still another time, etc. This could be the source of considerable confusion in the data.

2. Inferring Pairwise Probabilities

The second point revolves around suggested devices for estimating $P(x, y)$ empirically. The difficulty in making such estimates for many classes of alternatives is that if the pair (x, y) is presented several times we suspect that the first responses are remembered and color the answers to later presentations. In other words, the first few responses alter the value of $P(x, y)$ governing the later responses. Barring the creation of an adequate learning theory, the problem, then, is to devise dodges that allow us to estimate $P(x, y)$ without actually presenting the simple choice between x and y more than once. One suggestion (see, for example, Coombs [1958]) is to have the subject rank-order several finite subsets of U, these sets being so chosen that each pair of alternatives (x, y) appears a number of times. An obvious estimate of $P(x, y)$ is the number of times that x is ranked superior to y divided by the total number of times that the (x, y) pair occurred.

Although this estimate is the one that immediately comes to mind, it does not follow from the axioms of probability alone. In fact, plausible models of ranking behavior can be devised for which it is incorrect. For example, suppose that $\{x, y, z\}$ is given and that in ranking it the subject selects a pair of alternatives at random (probability $\frac{1}{3}$), compares them, and decides which he ranks higher. Then he picks one of these at random (probability $\frac{1}{2}$) and compares it with the third. If this does not produce a ranking, then he compares the remaining two. As an illustration, suppose he chooses (x, y) first. Suppose he places x superior to y, which he does with probability $P(x, y)$. Now suppose he chooses to compare x with z and that he ranks x superior to z, which he does with probability $P(x, z)$. He still does not have a ranking, so he compares y with z, and with probability $P(y, z)$ he places y above z. Assuming independence, the total probability involved is $\frac{1}{3}P(x, y)\frac{1}{2}P(x, z)P(y, z)$. This is but one of the six ways he can achieve the ranking $x > y > z$. Writing out all six and summing, we find that

$$R(x > y > z) = \tfrac{1}{3}P(x, y)P(y, z)[2P(x, z) + 1].$$

Thus

$$R(x > y > z) - R(z > x > y) = P(x, y)[P(x, z) + P(y, z) - 1]$$

$$R(y > x > z) - R(z > y > x) = P(y, x)[P(x, z) + P(y, z) - 1].$$

Solving,

$$P(x, y)$$

$$= \frac{R(x > y > z) - R(z > x > y)}{R(x > y > z) - R(z > x > y) + R(y > x > z) - R(z > y > x)}.$$

The "obvious" estimate is, of course,

$$P(x, y) = R(x > y > z) + R(x > z > y) + R(z > x > y).$$

It is reasonably clear that these two formulas give different results; nonetheless, a numerical example is given because it illustrates just how different they can be. We consider the two cases of ranking probabilities shown in Table 4. The two estimates are

$$\text{Case I. } P(x, y) = \frac{0.3 - 0.2}{0.3 - 0.2 + 0.2 - 0.2} = 1.00$$

$$P(x, y) = 0.3 + 0.1 + 0.2 \qquad = 0.60$$

$$\text{Case II. } P(x, y) = \frac{0.3 - 0.2}{0.3 - 0.2 + 0.2 - 0} = 0.33$$

$$P(x, y) = 0.3 + 0.1 + 0.2 \qquad = 0.60.$$

TABLE 4. Hypothetical Probabilities of Rankings of $\{x, y, z\}$

Ranking \ Case	I	II
$x > y > z$	0.3	0.3
$x > z > y$	0.1	0.1
$y > x > z$	0.2	0.2
$y > z > x$	0.0	0.2
$z > x > y$	0.2	0.2
$z > y > x$	0.2	0.0

It is clear, therefore, that a model for ranking behavior must be postulated before any particular estimation scheme is justified. We will show that the model suggested earlier justifies the "obvious" scheme.

Let $x \in T$ and let ρ denote a ranking of $T - \{x\}$. We denote by $x > \rho$ the ranking of T in which x appears first and in which the elements of $T - \{x\}$ are ranked according to ρ. If σ is a ranking of T, then let $R_T(\sigma)$ denote the probability of its occurring.

Ranking postulate.

$$R_{\{x, y\}}(x > y) = P(x, y)$$

$$R_T(x > \rho) = P_T(x)R_{T-\{x\}}(\rho).$$

Theorem 9. *Let R_S and P_S be defined for all $S \subset T$ and suppose that*

(i) *they satisfy the ranking postulate,*
(ii) *P_S satisfies axiom 1,*
(iii) *all pairwise discriminations are imperfect;*

then

$$P(x, y) = \sum_{\substack{\rho \text{ such} \\ \text{that } x > y}} R_T(\rho).$$

PROOF. We shall prove this by induction on the size of T. It is trivially true for $|T| = 2$. Suppose it is true for $|T| = n - 1$; then we show it is true for $|T| = n$. The estimate $P(x, y)$ consists of the sum of all probabilities of rankings in which x is judged superior to y, so by the ranking postulate it includes all cases in which x is judged best from T, none in which y is judged best, and when $z \neq x, y$ is judged best from T it includes exactly those in which x was placed superior to y in $T - \{z\}$. Since $|T - \{z\}| = n - 1$, we know by the induction hypothesis that each of the latter has a probability of $P(x, y)$ of occurring, so

$$\hat{P}(x, y) = P_T(x) + P(x, y) \sum_{z \in T - \{x,y\}} P_T(z).$$

But, by axiom 1.i and the probability axioms,

$$P_T(x) = P(x, y)[P_T(x) + P_T(y)],$$

so

$$\hat{P}(x, y) = P(x, y)[P_T(x) + P_T(y) + \sum_{z \in T - \{x,y\}} P_T(z)]$$

$$= P(x, y) \sum_{z \in T} P_T(z)$$

$$= P(x, y),$$

as asserted.

In all likelihood this theorem is of primary interest for $|T| = 3$ or 4. This is partly because balanced experimental designs are generally employed in which all subsets of a given size from U are ranked (in which case practical considerations dictate a small T) and partly because axiom 1 becomes more suspect as the size of the set gets larger (see section 5.B).

It should be noted that a plausible ranking model based on uncorrelated discriminal dispersions also leads to the natural estimate for $P(x, y)$; the proof is given for only three alternatives, but it can be generalized. Observe that by changing variables and integrating by parts we have

$$R(x > y > z) = \int_{-\infty}^{\infty} f_{u(x)}(t) \int_{\infty}^{0} f_{u(y)}(t - \tau) F_{u(z)}(t - \tau) \, d\tau \, dt$$

$$= \int_{-\infty}^{\infty} f_{u(x)}(t) \int_{-\infty}^{t} f_{u(y)}(r) F_{u(z)}(r) \, dr \, dt$$

$$= F_{u(x)}(t) \int_{-\infty}^{t} f_{u(y)}(r) F_{u(z)}(r) \, dr \Big]_{-\infty}^{\infty}$$

$$\qquad\qquad - \int_{-\infty}^{\infty} F_{u(x)}(t) f_{u(y)}(t) F_{u(z)}(t) \, dt$$

$$= P(y, z) - P_{\{x,y,z\}}(y).$$

So,

$$R(x > y > z) + R(x > z > y) + R(z > x > y)$$

$$= P(y, z) - P_{\{x,y,z\}}(y) + P(z, y) - P_{\{x,y\,z\}}(z) + P(x, y)$$

$$\qquad\qquad\qquad\qquad\qquad\qquad - P_{\{x,y,z\}}(x)$$

$$= P(x, y).$$

It is interesting that for three alternatives the ranking postulate, together with axiom 1, leads to the same expression for $R(x > y > z)$ as the discriminal dispersion model:

$$R(x > y > z) = P_{\{x,y,z\}}(x)P(y, z)$$
$$= [1 - P_{\{x,y,z\}}(y) - P_{\{x,y,z\}}(z)]P(y, z)$$
$$= P(y, z) - P_{\{x,y,z\}}(y).$$

This formal similarity between the models does not extend beyond three alternatives, as is easily seen by writing out the expressions for four alternatives. This result should not be interpreted as implying that the two ranking models are the same for three alternatives, since, if theorem 7 holds, the models are inconsistent.

Note added in proof: A model very similar to that introduced in section 1.F and employed in section 2.E to study signal detection and recognition has been proposed independently by R. N. Shepard ("Stimulus and response generalization: A stochastic model relating generalization to distance in psychological space," *Psychometrika*, **22,** 325–345, 1957) for the analysis of stimulus confusion, i.e., recognition. He postulates that the pairwise probabilities can be represented as in theorem 3 and that each scale value is the product of a "weight," which corresponds to our response bias, and a term exp $(-d_{ij})$, which corresponds to the confusion parameter ρ_{ij} employed in section 2.E.5. The quantity d_{ij} is interpreted as the "psychological distance" between stimuli i and j. In our terminology it corresponds to the absolute value of the difference between their Fechnerian (or Thurstonian) scale values. Shepard presents empirical tests of his model in "Stimulus and response generalization: Tests of a model relating generalization to distance in psychological space," *J. Exp. Psychol.*, **55,** 509–523, 1958.

chapter 3

APPLICATIONS

TO UTILITY THEORY

A. INTRODUCTION

The notion of the utility of money, and of other commodities, has long existed in economics. Although the problem can be of intrinsic interest to psychologists, it has concerned economists largely because of the mathematical convenience that would result were it possible to attach numbers to various commodities and commodity bundles in such a way that numerical magnitudes would reflect preferences. The discussion of scaling given in section 1.E and the proof (theorem 4) that a ratio scale exists under relatively weak conditions have probably made clear that I do not believe the utility problem to be inherently different from other scaling problems. For example, at least in principle, a person's utility for money can be determined by having him make comparisons between money and other alternatives with which and among which there are imperfect preference discriminations. The utility of money may be defined, just as money itself is, in terms of relations among other commodities. That is to say, there is little difference in the concept of utility and of money except that the former is defined entirely by a single individual, whereas the latter requires several interacting individuals and is, *ipso facto*, interpersonally comparable. Utility can be viewed as a private

75

money that allows for "internal bookkeeping," but just because it is private it need never be made tangible. It is dubious that many economists will be satisfied with this treatment, since among other things it forces them outside the algebraic framework traditionally used for the problem; but it should help serve to locate the issue for psychologists.

The purpose of this chapter is not to comment further upon the traditional utility problem, but rather partially to investigate the structure of a psychologically interesting problem that has arisen in a modern recasting of the utility notion. This is the problem of a person making choices among uncertain alternatives or, more familiarly, among gambles.

The traditional phrasing of the utility problem in terms of weakly ordered sets of alternatives led either to no numerical representation or simply to an ordinal scale. For much of modern decision theory—game theory and statistical decision theory—much more is needed to push through many of the more interesting results. The main property required is that in some sense the utility of a gamble should equal the expectation of its component utilities, and this implies an interval scale of utility. As von Neumann and Morgenstern [1947] first showed, we can in fact construct an algebraic choice theory for gambles, provided that the probabilities of the events are known, that leads to an interval scale of utility having the expected-utility property. This gives a possible, though in practice cumbersome, way of determining a person's utility for money and other commodities.

The main difficulties of their and related axiomatizations are three. First, they assume that subjects know and deal with the objective probabilities of the events as such, rather than with some subjective measure of likelihood. Why, one cannot help asking, should a subject distort the money scale but not the probability scale? Second, the axiomatic structure needed to get the desired interval scale postulates a degree of rationality and consistency for people that is a bit too quixotic to take entirely seriously. Third, laboratory subjects rather clearly exhibit a mixture of perfect and imperfect discriminations among gambles (see, for example, Mosteller and Nogee [1951]). This makes it difficult to verify and use the model, since such algebraic axiomatizations have not been equipped with handy error theories.

The work over the past decade and a half has been concerned with bypassing these difficulties in one way or another but always with some form of the expected-utility property as the guiding goal. Two reasons for clinging to this idea have probably been dominant: the need for it in decision theory if that field is not to become inordinately complex and the attractive simplicity of decomposing gambles into their two obvious components. Although it would be nice to cite experimental evidence as a third reason, it must be admitted that the data so far collected are most ambiguous. No survey of this theoretical work is attempted here, but mention should be made of several of the more important contributions. Savage [1954] showed that an algebraic axiomatization in terms of alternatives and events can be constructed which leads to a subjective probability function over events and a utility function over gambles. The former satisfies the usual probability axioms, the latter is an interval scale, and, together, they exhibit the expected utility property. This means that the first of the three difficulties is not inherent, but both the second and third remained in full force in Savage's work. Davidson, Suppes, and Siegel [1957], elaborating the earlier ideas of Ramsey [1931], separated the subjective probability and utility problems by working with events having subjective probability $\frac{1}{2}$. This means that certain equations arising from the expected-utility hypothesis can be reduced to equations involving only utilities because all the event terms are the same and so can be canceled. Once the utilities are ascertained, the subjective probabilities of other events can be calculated from the expected-utility hypothesis. Their axiomatization, which also places severe demands upon the consistency of the subjects, has the experimentally difficult feature of requiring pure alternatives that are "equally spaced in utility." Scattered attempts have been made to soften the second difficulty by introducing imperfect discrimination into the choices (see Block and Marschak [1957], Chipman [1957], Davidson and Marschak [1958], Georgescu-Roegen [1936, 1958], Luce [1958], Marschak [1955]) but none of them has dealt very successfully with the mixed perfect and imperfect discriminations that seem to occur.

We already know that if we choose to assume axiom 1 then we need not flinch at the latter problem; the only question is what sort of theory can be constructed. The purpose of the chapter is to investigate this question. Although scales are used incidentally, we will not be concerned with proving the existence of numerical scales of utility and subjective probability as such but rather with the beginnings of a possible descriptive theory of choices among uncertain alternatives. Since the problem is viewed as having inherent psychological interest and not simply as a necessary stepping stone for the study of other problems in decision theory and economics, we will not search for simple approximations that overlook the fine detail of the phenomenon. In particular, we will not be (mis)-guided by the organizing principle that has dominated most of modern utility theory: the expected-utility hypothesis. I have strong reservations about the detailed accuracy of this hypothesis, and I think that it can be argued that it has resulted in some sterility in an area of rich complexity.

B. DECOMPOSABLE PREFERENCE STRUCTURES

1. Definitions

Let A be a given set (of pure alternatives) and E a Boolean algebra (of chance events). A symbol of the form $a\rho b$, in which $a, b \in A$ and $\rho \in E$, is interpreted as the gamble (or uncertain alternative) in which a is the outcome if ρ occurs and b the outcome if it does not. Our total set of alternatives consists of these gambles plus the pure alternatives, i.e., the set $S(A, E) = (A \times E \times A) \cup A$.

Definition 5. *A decomposable preference structure $\langle A, E, P, Q \rangle$ is a system in which A is a set, E a Boolean algebra, P a family $\{P_T\}$ of probability measures defined for every $T \subset S(A, E)$ such that $|T| \leqq 3$, and Q a family $\{Q_D\}$ of probability measures defined for every $D \subset E$ such that $|D| \leqq 3$, for which the P_T's and Q_D's satisfy axiom 1 and*

Axiom 2. $P(a\rho b, a\sigma b) = P(a, b)Q(\rho, \sigma) + P(b, a)Q(\sigma, \rho)$, *for* $a, b \in A$ *and* $\rho, \sigma \in E$.

Of course, P_T should be interpreted as the probability of choice from the set of alternatives T according to the criterion of preference; the P_T's may be estimated directly from choice data. The Q_D's, which should be thought of as the probabilities of choice from subsets D of events according to the criterion of subjective likelihood, cannot be estimated directly; they must be inferred from axiom 2.

This axiom was introduced in Luce [1958], where it was called the "decomposition axiom" because it decomposes the discrimination between certain pairs of gambles into a discrimination between pure alternatives and one between events. It has much the same flavor as the expected-utility hypothesis, except that it is much weaker. An a priori rationalization of it can be developed by considering the conditions under which a subject should prefer the gamble $a\rho b$ to $a\sigma b$. If a is preferred to b, then he should choose the gamble in which a is the more likely outcome. So, if he deems ρ more likely to occur than σ, then he should choose $a\rho b$. On the other hand, if b is preferred to a, then he should choose the event that makes b more likely. Thus, if not-ρ, $\bar{\rho}$, is deemed more likely than $\bar{\sigma}$, i.e., if σ is deemed more likely than ρ, then $a\rho b$ is chosen. Now, by hypothesis, $P(a, b)$ is the probability that a is preferred to b and $Q(\rho, \sigma)$ is the probability that ρ is deemed more likely to occur than σ; so, if these two discriminations are independent, $P(a, b)Q(\rho, \sigma)$ is the probability of choosing $a\rho b$ in the first case. Similarly, $P(b, a)Q(\sigma, \rho)$ is the probability in the second, mutually exclusive case. The sum, therefore, must give $P(a\rho b, a\sigma b)$, and that is axiom 2. The crucial assumption in this argument is the statistical independence of the discrimination of preference from the discrimination of subjective likelihood. Some doubt that this is universally true; however, as yet, no compelling counter-intuitive example has been given and no conclusive data exist.

A binary relation on E is next defined that is similar to, but in general distinct from, the trace (definition 4, section 1.G.2). Nonetheless, the same notation is used since the trace does not play a role in the following discussion.

Definition 6. *If $\langle A, E, P, Q \rangle$ is a decomposable preference structure and $\rho, \sigma \in E$, then we write $\rho \gtrsim \sigma$ if and only if $Q(\rho, \sigma) \geq \frac{1}{2}$.*

2. The Principal Result

Experimental work in the utility and related areas strongly suggests two facts that have not fitted smoothly into the traditional models. First, subjects generally discriminate pure alternatives perfectly with respect to preference while, at the same time, imperfectly discriminating some (though not all) pairs of gambles. Second, instead of exhibiting behavior that would correspond to the existence of extremely finely graded scales over the alternatives and the events, subjects appear to group objects and events into categories which they are unable to refine to any great extent (see, e.g., Miller [1956]). The latter phenomenon, which may relate to and possibly explains the former, seems especially pronounced when it comes to events. One need introspect only a few seconds to conclude that he probably does not have a very refined scale of subjective likelihood over events, particularly over those for which objective probabilities are unknown and are not easily calculated.

The question of incorporating these two phenomena into a theory has seemed difficult. Previous theories have either completely excluded imperfect discrimination (e.g., the algebraic theories of utility) or completely excluded perfect discrimination (e.g., Thurstone's and other probability models). This, however, is not a problem in the present theory. Nevertheless, we appear to be left with the necessity of making *ad hoc* assumptions about which discriminations are perfect, and, as was pointed out in section 1.D.2, experimental evidence may not be a completely reliable guide in this matter. As to categories, how do they, rather than numerical scales, get into the model? The obvious tack of postulating them not only seems to prejudge the problem too much but is beset by questions of how many categories and where to locate their boundaries.

As is demonstrated in the next theorem, some of these difficulties are nicely bypassed in a decomposable preference structure. It is shown that either preference discrimination is perfect among pure alternatives or the events are categorized into, at most, three classes. In the latter case imperfect preference discrimination is narrowly prescribed (section 3.C.2). The interest of this result resides in the assumptions from which it follows—axioms 1 and 2—neither of which appears to possess any quality of discreteness, yet together they lead either to some cases of perfect discrimination or to a categorization of events. Although some feel that the particular theorem proved here will not stand before empirical data, its significance does not rest alone upon its empirical accuracy. It demonstrates conclusively the existence of a plausible axiomatization of behavior from which flow results about perfect discrimination and categorization. Presumably, if the present assumptions are wrong, others that are not very different can be found which are more nearly correct, and they may lead to similar results.

Theorem 10. *Let* $\langle A, E, P, Q \rangle$ *be a decomposable preference structure. If there exist* $a, b \in A$ *such that* $P(a, b) \neq 0, \frac{1}{2}$ *or* 1, *then the relation* $\sim$ *is an equivalence relation that partitions* E *into, at most, three equivalence classes.*

The proof of this result is given as a series of four lemmas, in each of which the hypotheses of theorem 10 are implicitly assumed to hold.

Lemma 5. *For distinct* $\rho, \sigma, \tau \in E$,

$$(K + 1)\{2[Q(\rho, \sigma) + Q(\sigma, \tau) + Q(\tau, \rho)] - 3\}$$
$$+ K^2[Q(\rho, \sigma)Q(\sigma, \tau)Q(\tau, \rho) - Q(\rho, \tau)Q(\tau, \sigma)Q(\sigma, \rho)] = 0,$$

where $K = \dfrac{P(a, b)}{P(b, a)} - 1$.

PROOF. Since $P(b, a) = 1 - P(a, b) \neq 0$ and $Q(\rho, \sigma) = 1 - Q(\sigma, \rho)$, axiom 2 may be rewritten as

$$P(a\rho b, a\sigma b) = P(b, a) \left\{1 + \left[\frac{P(a, b)}{P(b, a)} - 1\right] Q(\rho, \sigma)\right\}$$

$$= P(b, a)[1 + KQ(\rho, \sigma)].$$

Since $0 < P(a, b) < 1$, $P(a\rho b, a\sigma b) \neq 0$ or 1, hence, by theorem 2,

$$P(a\rho b, a\sigma b)P(a\sigma b, a\tau b)P(a\tau b, a\rho b) = P(a\rho b, a\tau b)P(a\tau b, a\sigma b)P(a\sigma b, a\rho b).$$

Substitute the above expression for the P's into the last equation and simplify, noting that $Q(\rho, \sigma) = 1 - Q(\sigma, \rho)$ and that $K \neq 0$. The assertion follows.

Lemma 6. $\gtrsim$ *is a weak ordering of* E.

PROOF. Since comparability and reflexivity are obvious, we need only establish transitivity. Suppose there exist ρ, σ, and τ such that $Q(\rho, \sigma) \geqq \frac{1}{2}$, $Q(\sigma, \tau) \geqq \frac{1}{2}$, and $Q(\rho, \tau) < \frac{1}{2}$. Since both $K + 1 > 0$ and $K^2 > 0$, lemma 5 implies

$$0 = (K + 1)\{2[Q(\rho, \sigma) + Q(\sigma, \tau) + Q(\tau, \rho)] - 3\}$$
$$+ K^2[Q(\rho, \sigma)Q(\sigma, \tau)Q(\tau, \rho) - Q(\rho, \tau)Q(\tau, \sigma)Q(\sigma, \rho)]$$
$$> (K + 1)\{2[\tfrac{1}{2} + \tfrac{1}{2} + \tfrac{1}{2}] - 3\} + K^2[\tfrac{1}{8} - \tfrac{1}{8}]$$
$$= 0.$$

As this is impossible, we must conclude that the relation is transitive.

It is an immediate consequence of lemma 6 that $\sim$ is an equivalence relation.

Lemma 7. *Suppose that for distinct* $\rho, \sigma, \tau \in E$, $Q(\rho, \sigma)$, $Q(\sigma, \tau)$, *and* $Q(\rho, \tau) \neq 0, 1$, *then either* $\rho \sim \sigma$, $\sigma \sim \tau$, *or* $\rho \sim \tau$.

PROOF. From theorem 2 we know that

$$Q(\rho, \sigma)Q(\sigma, \tau)Q(\tau, \rho) = Q(\rho, \tau)Q(\tau, \sigma)Q(\sigma, \rho),$$

so the second term of the equation in lemma 5 is 0. Since $K + 1 > 0$, it follows that

$$0 = [Q(\rho, \sigma) - \tfrac{1}{2}] + [Q(\sigma, \tau) - \tfrac{1}{2}] + [Q(\tau, \rho) - \tfrac{1}{2}].$$

By theorem 3, there exists a function v such that

$$Q(\rho, \sigma) = \frac{v(\rho)}{v(\rho) + v(\sigma)},$$

etc. Substituting these into the above expression and simplifying yields

$$[v(\rho) - v(\sigma)][v(\sigma) - v(\tau)][v(\tau) - v(\rho)] = 0,$$

so one term, say the first, is zero. In that case $Q(\rho, \sigma) = v(\rho)/2v(\rho) = \frac{1}{2}$, so $\rho \sim \sigma$.

Lemma 8. *The equivalence relation* $\sim$ *partitions* E *into at most three equivalence classes.*

PROOF. Suppose that there are at least four classes; let ρ, σ, τ, and ω be from distinct classes and ordered, say, $\rho > \sigma > \tau > \omega$. Consider the subset $\{\rho, \sigma, \tau\}$; then by lemma 7 either $Q(\rho, \sigma) = 1$, $Q(\sigma, \tau) = 1$, or $Q(\rho, \tau) = 1$. But suppose $Q(\rho, \sigma) = 1$ and $Q(\rho, \tau) < 1$; then by lemma 5 we have

$$0 = (K + 1)\{2[Q(\rho, \sigma) + Q(\sigma, \tau) + Q(\tau, \rho)] - 3\}$$
$$+ K^2[Q(\rho, \sigma)Q(\sigma, \tau)Q(\tau, \rho) - Q(\rho, \tau)Q(\tau, \sigma)Q(\sigma, \rho)]$$
$$> (K + 1)\{2[1 + \tfrac{1}{2} + 0] - 3\} + K^2[1\tfrac{1}{2}0 - 0]$$
$$= 0,$$

which is impossible, hence we may assume $Q(\rho, \tau) = 1$. A similar argument shows that $Q(\rho, \omega) = 1$. Using $\{\rho, \tau, \omega\}$ in lemma 5 therefore yields

$$0 = (K + 1)\{2[1 + Q(\tau, \omega) + 0] - 3\} + K^2 0,$$

hence $Q(\tau, \omega) = \frac{1}{2}$. Thus the supposition of four distinct classes is false.

Lemmas 6 and 8 prove theorem 10. An important property of these equivalence classes is stated in the next theorem.

Theorem 11. *Let $\langle A, E, P, Q \rangle$ be a decomposable preference structure having $a, b \in A$ such that $P(a, b) \neq 0, \frac{1}{2}$, or 1. If $\rho \sim \rho'$ and $\sigma \sim \sigma'$, where $\rho, \rho', \sigma, \sigma' \in E$, then $Q(\rho, \sigma) = Q(\rho', \sigma')$.*

PROOF. By lemma 5,

$$\begin{aligned}
0 &= (K + 1)\{2[Q(\rho, \rho') + Q(\rho', \sigma) + Q(\sigma, \rho)] - 3\} \\
&\quad + K^2[Q(\rho, \rho')Q(\rho', \sigma)Q(\sigma, \rho) - Q(\rho, \sigma)Q(\sigma, \rho')Q(\rho', \rho)] \\
&= (K + 1)\{2[\tfrac{1}{2} + Q(\rho', \sigma) + 1 - Q(\rho, \sigma)] - 3\} \\
&\quad + K^2\{\tfrac{1}{2}Q(\rho', \sigma)[1 - Q(\rho, \sigma)] - Q(\rho, \sigma)[1 - Q(\rho', \sigma)]\tfrac{1}{2}\} \\
&= [2(K + 1) + \tfrac{1}{2}K^2][Q(\rho', \sigma) - Q(\rho, \sigma)].
\end{aligned}$$

Observe that if $2(K + 1) + \frac{1}{2}K^2 = \frac{1}{2}(K + 2)^2 = 0$, then

$$\frac{P(a, b)}{P(b, a)} + 1 = K + 2$$

$$= 0,$$

so $P(a, b) = -P(b, a)$, which is impossible. Thus, $Q(\rho', \sigma) = Q(\rho, \sigma)$. In like manner $Q(\rho', \sigma') = Q(\rho', \sigma)$.

3. Discussion

In large measure the significance of the preceding results was discussed prior to proving them; however, two additional points can be made. If, in an experiment, a subject exhibits more than three classes of events, i.e., if there are events ρ, σ, τ, and ω such that

$$Q(\rho, \sigma) > \tfrac{1}{2}, \qquad Q(\sigma, \tau) > \tfrac{1}{2}, \qquad Q(\tau, \omega) > \tfrac{1}{2},$$

which adults generally seem to, then the occurrence of a single imperfect discrimination among pure alternatives is enough to show that the subject either does not satisfy axiom 1 or axiom 2. Further detailed analysis would be required to determine which one is violated. Of course, in experiments in which money outcomes are used, we anticipate that subjects will exhibit the perfect discriminations required by the assumptions.

Consider an organism that, throughout its life, satisfies the axioms of a decomposable preference structure, that initially does not discriminate pure alternatives perfectly, and that, during growth, gradually improves its discrimination of both alternatives and events. Then, according to theorem 10, it must initially categorize events into, at most, three classes, and it must achieve perfect preference discrimination among pure alternatives prior to refining its discrimination of events. Or, stated facetiously, desires must be perfected before judgments can be.

C. ADDITIONAL AXIOMS

1. Existence of Three Event Classes

To the axioms of a decomposable preference structure let us now add three more plausible axioms that are similar in spirit to axioms that are relatively standard in utility theory. From these we will show that if there are any cases of imperfect preference discrimination among pure alternatives then the events must be partitioned into exactly three classes. In all of these axioms it is assumed that a decomposable preference structure $\langle A, E, P, Q \rangle$ is given.

Axiom 3. *For $a, b \in A$, $\rho \in E$, and $x \in S(A, E)$,*

$$P(a\rho b, x) = P(b\bar{\rho}a, x),$$

where $\bar{\rho}$ denotes the complement of ρ.

In essence, this states that $a\rho b$ is not a different gamble from $b\bar{\rho}a$, which is not unreasonable, since in both a is the outcome when ρ occurs and b when it does not. The only doubts are empirical in origin. Operationally, the axiom states that the order of presentation of a gamble—either the temporal order of an oral presentation or the spatial order of a written presentation—does not affect the probability of choice. A priori this seems sensible, but the study of choice behavior in other areas, particularly psychophysics and attitude testing, has amassed an impressive aggregate of data which shows that order can make a difference (see section 1.F). Little is known about this phenomenon except that it exists, its general order of magnitude for some dimensions, and that *for some purposes* its effect can be bypassed by randomizing the order of presentation. It is quite possible, therefore, that we should devise theories in which axiom 3 is neither assumed nor a consequence.

Axiom 4. *There exist $a^*, b^* \in A$ such that $P(a^*, b^*) \neq \frac{1}{2}$ and $\rho^*, \sigma^* \in E$ such that $Q(\rho^*, \sigma^*) \neq \frac{1}{2}$.*

This is nothing more than a demand that the decomposable preference structure be nontrivial in the sense that the subject is neither indifferent among all of the alternatives nor among all of the events.   Empirically, the axiom is easily realized.

Lemma 9.   *If $\langle A, E, P, Q \rangle$ is a decomposable preference structure that satisfies axioms 3 and 4, then for $\rho, \sigma \in E$, $Q(\rho, \sigma) = Q(\bar{\sigma}, \bar{\rho})$.*

PROOF.   Let a^* and b^* be the elements postulated in axiom 4; then by axiom 3,

$$P(a^*\rho b^*, a^*\sigma b^*) = P(a^*\rho b^*, b^*\bar{\sigma}a^*)$$
$$= P(b^*\bar{\rho}a^*, b^*\bar{\sigma}a^*).$$

Apply axiom 2 to the first and last terms and simplify:

$$P(a^*, b^*)[Q(\rho, \sigma) - Q(\bar{\sigma}, \bar{\rho})] + P(b^*, a^*)[Q(\bar{\rho}, \bar{\sigma}) - Q(\sigma, \rho)] = 0.$$

Interchange the roles of a^* and b^*,

$$P(b^*, a^*)[Q(\rho, \sigma) - Q(\bar{\sigma}, \bar{\rho})] + P(a^*, b^*)[Q(\bar{\rho}, \bar{\sigma}) - Q(\sigma, \rho)] = 0.$$

By axiom 4, the determinant $P(a^*, b^*)^2 - P(b^*, a^*)^2 \neq 0$; hence $Q(\rho, \sigma) = Q(\bar{\sigma}, \bar{\rho})$.

Note that axiom 1 is not used in this proof.

Axiom 5.   *There exists at least one $\epsilon \in E$ such that $Q(\epsilon, \bar{\epsilon}) = \frac{1}{2}$.*

This postulates the existence of an event that is deemed by the subject to be no more or less likely to occur than its complement, i.e., an event with subjective probability equal to that of its complement.   It is never certain that a random collection of events will in fact include such an event, but, as Davidson, Suppes, and Siegel [1957] have demonstrated empirically, some exist.   (A flip of a coin is not one; there is a widespread bias in favor of heads.)

Theorem 12.   *Let $\langle A, E, P, Q \rangle$ be a decomposable preference structure which, in addition, satisfies axioms 3–5.   Either $P(a, b) = 0$, $\frac{1}{2}$, or 1, for all $a, b \in A$, or the equivalence relation $\sim$ partitions E into exactly three equivalence classes.*

The proof is divided into two lemmas, the hypotheses of the theorem and the existence of $a, b \in A$ such that $P(a, b) \neq 0$, $\frac{1}{2}$, or 1 being assumed in each.   Thus lemmas 5–9 and theorem 11 hold.

Lemma 10.   *If $\rho \sim \bar{\rho}$ and $\sigma \sim \bar{\sigma}$, then $\rho \sim \sigma$; and if $\rho \sim \bar{\rho}$ and $\sigma \sim \rho$, then $\sigma \sim \bar{\sigma}$.*

PROOF.   If $\rho \sim \bar{\rho}$ and $\sigma \sim \bar{\sigma}$, then by theorem 11, $Q(\rho, \sigma) = Q(\bar{\rho}, \bar{\sigma})$. By lemma 9, $Q(\bar{\rho}, \bar{\sigma}) = Q(\sigma, \rho)$, so $Q(\rho, \sigma) = Q(\sigma, \rho)$. This, with $Q(\rho, \sigma) + Q(\sigma, \rho) = 1$, implies $Q(\rho, \sigma) = \frac{1}{2}$, so $\rho \sim \sigma$.

If $\rho \sim \bar{\rho}$ and $\sigma \sim \rho$, then by lemma 6, $\sigma \sim \bar{\rho}$. But, since $\bar{\sigma} \sim \bar{\sigma}$, theorem

11 implies $Q(\sigma, \bar{\sigma}) = Q(\bar{\rho}, \bar{\sigma})$. However, lemma 9 and $\rho \sim \sigma$ imply $Q(\bar{\rho}, \bar{\sigma}) = Q(\sigma, \rho) = \frac{1}{2}$, so $\sigma \sim \bar{\sigma}$.

Lemma 11. *The equivalence relation $\sim$ partitions E into at least three equivalence classes.*

PROOF. Denote by $C(\frac{1}{2})$ the class containing event ϵ of axiom 5. By axiom 5, $\bar{\epsilon} \in C(\frac{1}{2})$. By lemma 10, $C(\frac{1}{2})$ consists exactly of those events ρ with the property that $\rho \sim \bar{\rho}$. By axiom 4, there exists an event $\rho^* \notin C(\frac{1}{2})$. Denote by $C(1)$ the class containing ρ^*. By lemmas 9 and 10, $\bar{\rho}^* \notin C(\frac{1}{2})$ and $\bar{\rho}^* \notin C(1)$, so there must be a third class $C(0)$ containing $\bar{\rho}^*$, which establishes that there are three classes.

Lemmas 8 and 11 prove theorem 12.

2. Restrictions on P(a, b)

It seems doubtful that there can be but three equivalence classes of events, and so we are forced to conclude that if a decomposable preference structure accurately describes them adults, at least, must discriminate perfectly among pure alternatives. In this section another result that reinforces this inference is shown.

Suppose that $\langle A, E, P, Q \rangle$ is a decomposable preference structure satisfying axioms 3–5 and that there exist $a, b \in A$ such that $P(a, b) \neq 0$, $\frac{1}{2}$, or 1; then by theorem 12 we know that E is partitioned into three equivalence classes. Let ρ, σ, and τ be representatives from them, ordered $\rho > \sigma > \tau$. By theorem 11 and lemmas 7 and 9, we know that

$$Q(\rho, \sigma) = Q(\sigma, \tau) = q \quad \text{and} \quad Q(\rho, \tau) = 1,$$

where q is some number, $\frac{1}{2} < q \leqq 1$. Substituting in lemma 5,

$$(K + 1)[2(q + q + 0) - 3] + K^2[0 - (1 - q)(1 - q)] = 0,$$

so

$$\frac{K + 1}{K^2} = \frac{(1 - q)^2}{4q - 3}.$$

Since $K + 1 > 0$ and $K^2 > 0$, it follows immediately that

$$\tfrac{3}{4} < q < 1.$$

Recalling that $K = \dfrac{P(a, b)}{P(b, a)} - 1$, we may solve the above equation:

$$P(a, b) = \frac{1}{2}\left[1 \pm \frac{(4q - 3)'}{2q - 1} \right].$$

Thus we see that if there are any cases of imperfect discrimination among pure alternatives their probabilities $(>\frac{1}{2})$ are all equal and they are uniquely determined by the probabilities of choice among the equivalence class of events. There is comparatively little freedom for imperfect discrimination in a decomposable preference structure satisfying axioms 3–5, and what there is is bought at the price of but three equivalence classes of events.

D. A PROPOSED EXPERIMENT

1. A Prediction

So far, we have introduced the idea of a decomposable preference structure as a possible model for an individual making choices among uncertain alternatives, and we have established one of its important properties. It is a plausible model in that there are some reasons for supposing that both axiom 1 and the decomposition axiom may be approximately true in some contexts. The model not only admits the possibility of mixed perfect and imperfect discriminations but to all intents requires them to be perfect among pure alternatives without at the same time demanding perfect discriminations among all gambles. We could leave it at that, noting that in principle the validity of the model can be checked completely, since both of the axioms refer only to observables. However, in practice such an experimental study would be monumental, since, to be at all persuasive, the estimates of the probabilities would have to be extremely accurate. That means enormous sample sizes, which in turn means a dreadfully long experiment—many months of observations on each subject. Thus no satisfactory test of the model is likely to be carried out unless we can find a consequence that is (1) qualitative and comparatively easy to detect in the laboratory, (2) different from the predictions of other models in this general area, and, hopefully, (3) different from the dictates of common sense. Fortunately, such a prediction—one that is easy to derive—can be made.

Theorem 13. *Suppose that $\langle A, E, P, Q \rangle$ is a decomposable preference structure, that a, b, c, d $\in$ A and ρ, σ $\in$ E are such that*

$$P(a, b) = P(c, d) = 1$$

and that all pairwise discriminations in the set

$$T = \{a\rho b, a\sigma b, c\rho d, c\sigma d\}$$

are imperfect, then

$$P(a\rho b, c\rho d) = P(a\sigma b, c\sigma d).$$

PROOF. By the decomposition axiom and the fact that $P(a, b) = P(c, d) = 1$,

$$P(a\rho b, a\sigma b) = Q(\rho, \sigma) = P(c\rho d, c\sigma d).$$

By theorem 4, there exists a positive ratio scale over T such that

$$P(a\rho b, a\sigma b) = \cfrac{1}{1 + \cfrac{v(a\sigma b)}{v(a\rho b)}}$$

and

$$P(c\rho d, c\sigma d) = \cfrac{1}{1 + \cfrac{v(c\sigma d)}{v(c\rho d)}}.$$

Equating these,

$$\frac{v(a\sigma b)}{v(a\rho b)} = \frac{v(c\sigma d)}{v(c\rho d)},$$

or, rewriting,

$$\frac{v(c\rho d)}{v(a\rho b)} = \frac{v(c\sigma d)}{v(a\sigma b)}.$$

From this and theorem 4, the conclusion follows immediately.

2. Experimental Implication

Let us examine an implication of this result. The choices involved are those discussed by Ramsey [1931] and Davidson, Suppes, and Siegel [1957], namely, those of the one-person game

	Option 1	Option 2
ρ	a	c
$\bar{\rho}$	b	d

in which the subject chooses the column and the chance event ρ selects the row. As far as is known, the only empirical study of such games is given in Davidson, Suppes, and Siegel [1957], but they varied a, b, c, and d while restricting ρ to be an event having subjective probability $\frac{1}{2}$ (i.e., an event satisfying axiom 5). Our theorem is concerned with at least two events, neither necessarily satisfying axiom 5. If a is preferred to b and c to d, and if we hold these payoffs fixed, the theorem says that as we vary the events we may find that the options are always perfectly discriminated; but—and this is the important point—if we do find any cases of imperfect discrimination, then they must appear in clusters, each cluster having a constant probability. Furthermore, there is no reason to suppose that any of these probabilities is $\frac{1}{2}$ or that they are symmetrically located about $\frac{1}{2}$. Thus, schematically, our data should exhibit the step-function pattern drawn in Figure 7.

It is clear that a transition from 0 to 1 probability of choice will occur only if one column does not dominate the other, i.e., only if $a > c$ and $d > b$ or $b > d$ and $c > a$, so we would study one of these cases.

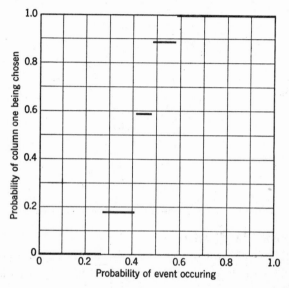

Figure 7. A typical step function predicted by the axioms of a decomposable preference structure for the probability of choosing column one in certain 2 x 2 payoff matrices.

As far as is known, no other theory predicts such a phenomenon, and there are those who consider it counter to common sense, feeling either that perfect discrimination will always be found, or, barring that, that the data will exhibit something like the traditional ogive of psychophysics. Unfortunately, there are no published data concerning such choices, but they should not be impossibly difficult to collect, since the qualitative nature of the prediction is sufficiently gross that extremely precise estimates of the probabilities are probably not needed.

3. A Utility Decomposition

In theorem 13 we have considered only the case where $P(a, b) = P(c, d) = 1$, which in practice has been much less often studied than payoff matrices in which the larger entries are on the main diagonal. The question now is what we can say when $P(a, b) = P(d, c) = 1$. Note that the answer, given in theorem 14, does not lead to a striking empirical test; however, as is shown in section 4.F.2, the result is not without its uses.

Theorem 14. *Suppose that $\langle A, E, P, Q \rangle$ is a decomposable preference structure which satisfies axiom 3, that $a, b, c, d \in A$ and $\rho, \sigma \in E$ are such that*

$$P(a, b) = P(d, c) = 1$$

and that all pairwise discriminations in the set

$$T = \{a\rho b,\ a\sigma b,\ c\rho d,\ c\sigma d\}$$

are imperfect, then

$$v(a\rho b)v(d\bar{\rho}c) = v(a\sigma b)v(d\bar{\sigma}c).$$

PROOF. By axiom 2, $P(a\rho b, a\sigma b) = Q(\rho, \sigma) = P(c\sigma d, c\rho d)$. So by theorem 4,

$$\frac{v(a\sigma b)}{v(a\rho b)} = \frac{v(c\rho d)}{v(c\sigma d)},$$

and the result follows from axiom 3.

If we apply theorems 13 and 14, respectively, to

$$
\begin{array}{cc}
 & \begin{array}{cc} 1 & 2 \end{array} \\
\begin{array}{c} \rho \\ \bar{\rho} \end{array} & \begin{bmatrix} a & c \\ b & d \end{bmatrix}
\end{array}
\quad \text{and} \quad
\begin{array}{cc}
 & \begin{array}{cc} 1 & 2 \end{array} \\
\begin{array}{c} \rho \\ \bar{\rho} \end{array} & \begin{bmatrix} a & d \\ b & c \end{bmatrix}
\end{array},
$$

in which $P(a, b) = P(c, d) = 1$, then for events ρ and σ we have the two equations

$$\frac{v(a\rho b)}{v(c\rho d)} = \frac{v(a\sigma b)}{v(c\sigma d)}$$

and

$$v(a\rho b)v(d\bar{\rho}c) = v(a\sigma b)v(d\bar{\sigma}c).$$

This suggests that v may be of the form

$$v(a\rho b) = w(a, b)\phi(\rho),$$

where ϕ is defined by

$$Q(\rho, \sigma) = \frac{\phi(\rho)}{\phi(\rho) + \phi(\sigma)}$$

and

$$\phi(\rho)\phi(\bar{\rho}) = \text{constant}.$$

If so, then, we have a local decomposition of the v-scale into a part that depends only upon the alternatives and a part that depends only upon the event, and this decomposition is consistent with the independence-of-unit condition (section 1.F).   Furthermore, it is similar in spirit to, although inherently different from, the expected utility hypothesis.   In addition, this form for v means that

$$P(a\rho b, c\rho d) = \frac{w(a, b)}{w(a, b) + w(c, d)};$$

hence the step function described in theorem 13 can have only one step intermediate between 0 and 1.

chapter 4

APPLICATIONS

TO LEARNING

A. INTRODUCTION

So far, choice behavior has been dealt with as if it were a static phenomenon, and only those situations have been considered in which some
care is usually taken to ensure that, to a first approximation, behavior is
not undergoing changes in time. Since, however, most choice patterns
are dynamic, exhibiting those somewhat systematic changes that result
from experience, we are almost bound to try to create a reasonable learning
theory that is consistent with our static choice theory. The essence of
what we shall do is to suppose that at any "instant" the static restraint
embodied in axiom 1 holds, while from instant to instant, or trial to trial,
systematic changes in the probabilities occur. That is to say, axiom 1
is *assumed* to be an invariant under the process of learning, even though its
constituent probabilities are undergoing changes.

The type of model that is developed falls under the general heading of
stochastic models of learning, which have recently been under active
investigation. The structure of these models is sketched here briefly, but
the reader who is unfamiliar with them is advised to consult Bush and
Mosteller [1955].

The organism is assumed to be confronted on each of a number of trials by the same finite set T of alternatives. It is customary to label the alternatives 1, 2, $\cdots$, i, $\cdots$, r and the trials 1, 2, $\cdots$, n, $\cdots$. His choice among the alternatives on a particular trial, say n, is assumed to be governed by a probability distribution that is peculiar to the trial. We may, therefore, denote the probability that he chooses alternative i from T on trial n by $P_T^{(n)}(i)$. A particular choice is made, at which point the environment responds to the organism in ways that can be thought of as rewarding or punishing him. Because of his preferences among outcomes it is reasonable to assume that the environmental outcome has some influence upon his tendency to make one choice or another on the next trial, i.e., it partially determines the probability distribution $P_T^{(n+1)}$. No assumption need be made now concerning the way the environment selects the outcome: it may or may not be contingent upon the organism's choice, and it may or may not depend upon chance. It is sufficient to suppose that whatever choice-outcome pair occurs there is some systematic modification of the choice probabilities.

Schematically, then, we have a set of trials, a set of alternatives, and a set of possible outcomes associated with each of the alternatives. For each trial there is a probability distribution over the alternatives which depends in some fashion upon the distributions that existed on preceding trials and upon the choice-outcome events that have already occurred. At this level of generality the model is able to encompass almost any experiment that traditionally has been labeled learning, provided only that discrete trials are defined. And for this reason it is totally incapable of predicting anything. This is not surprising, since we have not yet made any assumptions about learning (except that it depends upon both past events and the organism, which seems essential if we are to call it learning). The problem now is to specify explicitly how the probability distribution on any trial depends upon what has gone before.

The most important assumption that is usually made (in some current work it is being modified) is that $P_T^{(n+1)}$ depends only upon $P_T^{(n)}$ and upon the choice-outcome event that occurs on trial n. This is known as the *independence-of-path* assumption. It means, mathematically, that there is an operator that transforms the distribution on trial n into the distribution on trial $n + 1$. Its mathematical form depends, in general, upon both the choice made and the outcome on trial n, but it does not in fact depend upon the trial number n. Or, put another way, the operator does not depend upon the previous history of the organism, except to the extent that this is summarized by the probability distribution. If the organism happens to have the same distributions on trials 10 and 23, if he makes the same choice on each of these trials, and if the outcome is the same, then the distributions on trials 11 and 24 will be identical. Given that this assumption is true, there is no loss of generality in suppressing the trial number n and simply denoting the probabilities of the "present" trial by $P_T(i)$ and those of the "succeeding" trial by $P'_T(i)$.

The importance of the independence-of-path assumption can hardly be overstressed. It implies, for example, two related facts. First, the mathematical properties of the model are vastly simpler than they would otherwise be. Second, data from all of the trials can be used to obtain information about the operators, thus making it possible to obtain adequate information from a relatively small number of organisms.

Although no documentation will be attempted, it appears safe to say that to date the evidence is insufficient to reject the independence-of-path assumption for animal experiments, but with respect to human choice experiments many people have questioned the validity of the assumption. If the human data force us to abandon path independence, as they seem to, there can be no question that its substitute will have to be selected with great care if anything like a manageable theory is to result.

Accepting path independence, as we shall in a certain sense to be specified later, there still remains the question: what is the precise mathematical form of the operators? So far, any mathematical function that transforms a probability distribution into a probability distribution is a possibility, and that leaves us with much too much flexibility. In fact, absolutely no consequences of significance can be derived, and it is next to impossible to analyze data directly to find out what form the operators have. Some intelligent choice must be made. Largely for reasons of mathematical simplicity, but also because of a stimulus-sampling rationale given by Estes[1] and because of a philosophical rationale known as the combining-of-classes condition,[2] the operators have generally been assumed to be linear functions, i.e., of the form

$$P'_T(i) = \alpha_i P_T(i) + (1 - \alpha_i)\lambda_i.$$

By and large, the theoretical research has concentrated on calculating some of the statistical properties of this linear model, mainly for T's having two alternatives, and applying it to learning data.

B. RESPONSE STRENGTH OPERATORS

Most psychologists who have criticized the linear stochastic model have concentrated upon its questionable ability to handle certain empirical phenomena, and only to a lesser extent have they worried about its foundations. It has, however, been argued that the stimulus conditioning

---

[1] See Estes [1950], Bush and Mosteller [1951], or Chapter 2 of Bush and Mosteller [1955].

[2] See Chapter 1 of Bush and Mosteller [1955] or, for a more detailed discussion, Bush, Mosteller, and Thompson [1954].

rationale for the linear operators is none too convincing, and the combining-of-classes condition has also been questioned, since it assumes that the alternatives are arbitrary conventions of the experimenter, not empirically crucial distinctions made by the organism.   One of the more frustrating features of this modern approach to learning is the apparent conceptual disparity between it and the models that have been created to describe static choices, namely the psychophysical and psychometric models.   Somehow, if there is in fact a mathematical structure to choice behavior, there should be something in common between the static and dynamic theories.

One connection suggests itself.   The more traditional learning theorists (among others, Hull [1952] and Spence [1956]) have held that a distinction should be made between the strength or intensity of a response and the observed likelihood of that response.   For example, a 50–50 decision between two objectionable alternatives is not exactly the same as a 50–50 decision between two desirable ones (Miller [1944]).   If there were a numerical measure of the strength of a response, then this distinction might afford a basis for reconciling the stochastic models of learning and the ideas of psychophysical and psychometric scaling in such a way that a theory of the type desired by the behavior theorists would result. Although they have utilized the concept of response strength quite generally and have amassed an impressive body of related empirical data, their attempts to cast these notions into a mathematical framework have not yet resulted in a really satisfactory axiomatization.

An alternative resolution of these two classes of theories is suggested by theorems 3 and 4.   Although most experimental studies of learning involve a fixed set of alternatives throughout, we need not conclude that a theory of learning must limit itself to the given set of alternatives of a particular experiment.   A theory of behavior presumably describes an organism, not an experiment; and it is the theory of the organism, coupled with the "boundary conditions" imposed by the experiment, that should lead to experimental predictions.   There is no reason, a priori, to suppose that an organism could not have been confronted with a subset or a superset of the alternatives actually used, or, for that matter, that the set of alternatives could not be reduced or augmented midway through a run of trials.   Accepting this argument, then axiom 1 is not without meaning when applied to a single trial in the experiment.   If it is satisfied for T and its subsets, and if all pairwise discriminations are imperfect, then by theorem 3 (or 4) we know that the v-scale exists and that

$$P_T(i) = \frac{v(i)}{\sum\limits_{j \in T} v(j)}.$$

It is clear that if all v's are multiplied by the same positive constant, the probability distribution is unchanged.   So if we are willing to identify v with the intuitive idea of response strength, the over-all level of strength can change without necessarily altering the probability distribution. Put another way, the vector of scale values $\mathbf{v} = [v(1), v(2), \cdots, v(r)]$ uniquely determines the probability distribution, but the distribution determines $\mathbf{v}$ only up to multiplication by positive constants.

This asymmetry suggests, much as the behavior theorists have argued, that the v-scale may be more basic than the probabilities of response and that a learning model should be phrased in terms of changes of v-scale values which indirectly alter the probability distributions.   In fact, for two alternatives Thurstone [1930] and Gulliksen [1953] have postulated exactly this, treating the scale values as response strengths in their learning models.   Accepting such a model of learning, we are led to assume that the independence-of-path assumption holds for the v's, though it need no longer necessarily hold for the P's.   If so, then a particular alternative-outcome pair will effect a change that can be represented by a (vector) operator f of the form

$$\mathbf{v}' = f(\mathbf{v}).$$

The main problem is to decide what mathematical form to assume for f. There are various ways to approach this problem, including the assumption of a simple form because it is simple, but following the general spirit of this book we shall attack it axiomatically.   This development is broken down into two parts.   A pair of axioms is given which seem inescapable but which fail to define f sufficiently narrowly for the purpose of fitting data.   What other axioms to impose seems less clear-cut, and so three different possibilities are considered that lead to three different models, dubbed alpha, beta, and gamma.

The two less controversial restraints are the positiveness and independence-of-unit conditions.

Positiveness condition.

For all $\mathbf{v} > \mathbf{0}$, *where* $\mathbf{0}$ *is the null vector with r components,*

$$f(\mathbf{v}) > \mathbf{0}.$$

Since scale values are positive and since f is a mapping of a vector of scale values into a vector of scale values, this condition must be met.

The second condition to be imposed is a slight generalization of the independence-of-unit condition first introduced and discussed in section 1.F.1.   Recall that the argument supposes that the occurrence of some event results in a transformation of a v-scale value.   Since the unit of the ratio scale is unknowable, the mathematical form of the transformation should be independent of the unit.   Here the condition is extended to hold for transformations of the vector **v**, to which the same intuitive argument applies.

Independence-of-unit condition.

For all **v** > 0 *and for all real* $k > 0$,

$$f(k\mathbf{v}) = kf(\mathbf{v}).$$

C. ALPHA MODEL

The first special model to be considered is included largely to show that the present formulation is not inconsistent with the great body of work so far completed in stochastic learning theory.   However, it seems more difficult to make plausible the assumptions that appear to be needed to derive the traditional linear operators than to defend certain other assumptions, offered in the following two sections, which lead to different operators.   It may be that other, more intuitively compelling axioms can be found from which the linear operators follow, but none has yet been suggested.

The first condition was previously employed in section 1.F.1:

Unboundedness assumption.

For each alternative, any positive real number is a possible v-scale value.

This assumption is also made in the second model; however, in section 4.E what happens when it is denied to the extent that the v-scale is bounded from above is investigated.

Consider two vectors **v** and **v*** of response strengths; these are transformed into $f(\mathbf{v})$ and $f(\mathbf{v}^*)$.   Of course, the vector **v** + **v*** is transformed into $f(\mathbf{v} + \mathbf{v}^*)$.   It certainly would be pleasant if the effect of the learning experience on **v** + **v*** were the simple sum of the effects on **v** and on **v*** separately, in which case we would have the following property:

Superposition assumption.

For all **v**, **v*** > 0,

$$f(\mathbf{v} + \mathbf{v}^*) = f(\mathbf{v}) + f(\mathbf{v}^*).$$

Setting **v** = **v** and **v*** $= f(\mathbf{v}) - \mathbf{v}$ in this equation we see that

$$f[f(\mathbf{v})] = f[f(\mathbf{v}) - \mathbf{v}] + f(\mathbf{v}),$$

which has the following interpretation: two successive learning experiences of the same type are the same as one of that type plus the effect of the second on the increment of change induced by the first. Although this does not seem entirely convincing, no sharp counter example has yet been suggested.

It is well known that the unboundedness assumption, the superposition assumption, and the independence-of-unit condition constitute the definition of a linear transformation in a vector space, and to each such transformation there corresponds a matrix $[a_{ij}]$ such that

$$v'(i) = \sum_{j=1}^{r} a_{ij}v(j).$$

By the positiveness condition, $a_{ij} > 0$ for $i, j \in T$.

Observe that, in general, $P'_T(i)$ cannot be expressed as a linear combination of the $P_T(j)$. But let us postulate the following assumption:

Proportional change assumption.

There exists a constant $a > 0$ such that

$$\sum_{i=1}^{r} v'(i) = a \sum_{i=1}^{r} v(i).$$

Then,

$$P'_T(i) = \frac{v'(i)}{\sum_{i=1}^{r} v'(i)}$$

$$= \frac{\sum_{j=1}^{r} a_{ij}v(j)}{a \sum_{i=1}^{r} v(i)}$$

$$= \sum_{j=1}^{r} \frac{a_{ij}}{a} \frac{v(j)}{\sum_{i=1}^{r} v(i)}$$

$$= \sum_{j=1}^{r} \frac{a_{ij}}{a} P_T(j),$$

which is the desired linear expression.

The model defined by these five conditions will be referred to as the *alpha model;* it has been discussed quite fully by Bush and Mosteller in

their book.   It has the interesting features that it is linear and satisfies
the independence-of-path assumption both at the level of response
strengths (the v-scale) and at the level of behavioral probabilities.

Of these last two special assumptions, the former is quite familiar and
probably needs no further discussion.   The latter seems peculiar and
decidedly nonintuitive, but it is needed if the change in the probability
distribution is to be expressed simply as a linear combination of the probabilities on the preceding trial.   At the level of the v-scale it has the following effect: each operator results in a $\mathbf{v}'$-vector, the sum of whose components
is simply a constant times the sum of the components of the $\mathbf{v}$-vector.
That is to say, each operator changes the total sum of response strengths
by a fixed proportion.   Of course, each event, i.e., response-outcome
pair, has its own multiplicative constant.

Two somewhat shaky arguments can be given for this condition.   If
the organism is assumed to have a fixed amount of response strength
distributed over the alternatives, then learning can only redistribute it,
which means that the proportional change assumption holds with $a = 1$.
Alternatively, some have conjectured that the inverse of the choice reaction time is proportional to the total sum of response strengths, in which
case, if each environmental event can be assumed to have a proportional
effect on the reaction time, the sum of the response strengths has to be
changed by a constant proportion.   A better argument than these is
needed.

We observe that the proportional change assumption implies $\sum\limits_{i=1}^{r} a_{ij} = a$.
This follows from the fact that

$$\sum_{i=1}^{r} v'(i) = \sum_{i=1}^{r} \sum_{j=1}^{r} a_{ij} v(j)$$

$$= a \sum_{j=1}^{r} v(j),$$

so

$$\sum_{j=1}^{r} \left[\sum_{i=1}^{r} a_{ij} - a \right] v(j) = 0. \tag{1}$$

Since $v(j) > 0$, it is clear either that $\sum\limits_{i=1}^{r} a_{ij} = a$ or that, for at least one j,

$\sum\limits_{i=1}^{r} a_{ij} - a < 0$.   But then, by the unboundedness assumption, we can choose $v(j)$ sufficiently large and the other $v(i)$ sufficiently near 0 so that equation 1 is violated.

To illustrate how the present parameters relate to those usually used, consider $r = 2$. In the usual notation

$$P'(1, 2) = \alpha P(1, 2) + (1 - \alpha)\lambda.$$

In the present notation

$$P'(1, 2) = \frac{a_{11}}{a} P(1, 2) + \frac{a_{12}}{a} P(2, 1)$$

$$= \frac{(a_{11} - a_{12})}{a} P(1, 2) + \frac{a_{12}}{a}.$$

Thus,

$$\alpha = \frac{a_{11} - a_{12}}{a}$$

and

$$\lambda = \frac{a_{12}}{a(1 - \alpha)}$$

$$= \frac{a_{12}}{a - a_{11} + a_{12}}$$

$$= \frac{a_{12}}{a_{12} + a_{21}}.$$

D. BETA MODEL

1. Axiomatic Derivation

Within the reasonable limitations of the positiveness and independence-of-unit-conditions a second direction may be taken, leading to a new operator that is interesting because it is based upon assumptions that, to my mind, are fairly plausible. Recall that one way to arrive at the alpha model (Bush, Mosteller, and Thompson [1954]) is to impose the combining-of-classes condition. That argument leads to the conclusion that for a given choice-outcome pair the resulting probability, $P'_T(i)$, for alternative i depends upon $P_T(i)$, but not upon the rest of the original distribution. For $r = 2$ this is, in a sense, trivially true, and so the considerable success of the alpha model in that case cannot really be taken as a confirmation of this property. Nonetheless, it is intuitively compelling: the strength of alternative i, and its change in strength as a result of experience, undoubtedly depends upon its relation to the other alternatives, but it should not depend upon the relative strengths of these other alternatives one to another.   It is, therefore, a property not unlike Arrow's "independence of irrelevant alternatives," in which the effect of learning upon the probability of one alternative is not dependent upon the relative propensities of choice among the others.   For the reasons given in section 1.C.2, Arrow's term seems misleading, and we shall again use the modified term.

Independence-from-irrelevant-alternatives assumption.

For each choice-outcome pair, the vector operator f shall consist of r components, each of the general form

$$v'(i) = f_i[v(i)],$$

where $i \in T$.

The model defined by the positiveness and independence-of-unit conditions and the unboundedness and independence-from-irrelevant-alternatives assumptions will be called the *beta model*.

The independence-from-irrelevant-alternatives assumption allows us to employ the independence-of-unit condition and the unboundedness assumption exactly as we did in section 1.F.1; hence we know that

$$f_i(v) = \beta_i v.$$

By the positiveness condition, we know that $\beta_i > 0$.   Thus the form of the beta-model operator is completely determined.   It will be noted that $\beta_i > 1$ effects an increase in v, whereas $\beta_i < 1$ effects a decrease; these may be identified with reward and nonreward (or punishment) of the response, if we so desire.   Of course, $\beta_i = 1$ is the identity operator.

When more than one operator, i.e., when more than one choice-outcome event, is under consideration, three subscripts are needed on the β's.   For example, β_{xij} can be used to denote the operator that is applied to alternative j when alternative i was chosen and outcome x occurred.

As is easily seen, the beta model is a special case of the general matrix model (i.e., the one not satisfying the proportional-change assumption) in which the matrix is diagonal.

Put in probability terms, the beta operator becomes

$$P'_T(i) = \frac{\beta_i v(i)}{\sum_{j=1}^{r} \beta_j v(j)}.$$

By the definition of $v(i)$ in theorem 3, this reduces to

$$P'_T(i) = \frac{\beta_i P_T(i)}{\sum\limits_{j=1}^{r} \beta_j P_T(j)},$$

a nonlinear operator of the classical type in which path independence is met at the level of the probabilities as well as at the level of the v-scale. In section 4.E an operator is discussed for which this is not the case.

Note that these operators are commutative; this can be checked directly or inferred from the trivial fact that commutativity holds in the v-scale.

2. Simple Beta Model

For practical applications there are too many parameters in the general beta model. For example, with r alternatives and m outcomes per alternative, there are $r^2 m$. Let us, therefore, attempt to reduce their number. In much the same spirit as the independence-from-irrelevant-alternatives assumption, the argument can be made that if i is the alternative chosen learning should affect the response strength of i but not of the other, temporarily irrelevant alternatives. Stated in terms of probabilities, the relative chance of choice among the other alternatives should not be affected by the consequences resulting from the choice of i. Suppressing the choice and outcome subscripts, we have

$$\beta_i = \beta$$
$$\beta_j = 1, \qquad j \neq i.$$

This will be called the *simple beta model*. Another argument in favor of this model is given in section 4.F. The corresponding probability operators are

$$P'_T(i) = \frac{\beta P_T(i)}{\sum\limits_{\substack{j=1 \\ j \neq i}}^{r} P_T(j) + \beta P_T(i)}$$

$$= \frac{\beta P_T(i)}{1 + (\beta - 1)P_T(i)},$$

and

$$P'_T(j) = \frac{P_T(j)}{1 + (\beta - 1)P_T(i)}, \qquad j \neq i.$$

In the case of just two alternatives the form becomes slightly simpler:

$$P'(1, 2) = \frac{\beta P(1, 2)}{1 + (\beta - 1)P(1, 2)}$$

$$P'(2, 1) = \frac{P(2, 1)}{\beta - (\beta - 1)P(2, 1)}.$$

For two alternatives we note that there is no real distinction between the general and simple beta models, since

$$P'(1, 2) = \frac{\beta_1 P(1, 2)}{\beta_1 P(1, 2) + \beta_2 P(2, 1)}$$

$$= \frac{\dfrac{\beta_1}{\beta_2} P(1, 2)}{1 + \left(\dfrac{\beta_1}{\beta_2} - 1\right) P(1, 2)}.$$

These operators are in many ways similar to those studied by Bush, Estes, Mosteller, and others, except that they are nonlinear in the probabilities; however, they are linear in the v's, and that seems to be some compensation, especially since there is no additive constant.   This means that they are commutative, which makes some computations very easy. Unfortunately, in the analysis so far attempted this has seemed to be largely an illusory compensation.   It has not been possible to calculate any stochastic properties of the simple beta model—let alone of the general one—that can be used to estimate parameters.   The reason is that no interesting property appears to be defined in terms of the v's alone, the level at which the model is linear.   The probabilities of choice inevitably enter into the calculations.   These analytic difficulties, which hopefully are only temporary, are a decided inconvenience, since they make it extremely difficult to see what novel consequences can be predicted.   And so it is not easy to know how to make really significant tests of the model. Nevertheless, not all empirical work is blocked; there are various numerical procedures at our disposal.   An illustration is discussed in the next section.

3. Testing the Two-Alternative Beta Model

Since the alpha model has been successfully fitted to a considerable amount of learning data, particularly animal data, another model can be considered seriously only if it is equally successful.   And when the new model is as computationally difficult as the beta model, it had better be both extremely plausible and account for some data not adequately handled by the alpha model.   It is too early to judge whether the beta

model meets these empirical criteria; however, one application of the
beta model to data exists, which we will examine briefly. The experiment was performed and analyzed in terms of the alpha model by Galanter
and Bush [1959], and Bush [1957] carried out the beta model analysis of
these data. He has given me permission to discuss these unpublished
results here.

The experiment: Twenty rats were run for 192 trials in a T-maze.
During the first 48 trials a food reward was presented at every trial on one
side of the maze and no reward on the other side; at the 49th trial the
reward pattern was reversed and remained unchanged throughout the
second block of 48 trials. It was reversed twice more, but only the second
block of 48 trials is dealt with here.

If we let P denote the probability of going to the nonrewarded side,
then the two-commuting operator alpha model is described by the
equations:

$$P' = \begin{cases} \alpha_1 P + 1 - \alpha_1, & \text{if rewarded side is chosen} \\ \alpha_2 P + 1 - \alpha_2, & \text{if nonrewarded side is chosen.} \end{cases}$$

In addition to α_1 and α_2, the initial probability P_0 is a parameter of this
model. The value of P_0 is near 0, but it is difficult to obtain a precise
estimate; however, the alpha model is not unduly sensitive to small
changes of P_0 near 0 and because certain tables exist for $P_0 = 0$ it was
decided to use this as the estimate. Explicit expressions were developed
for the expected number of trials before the first success (choice of the
rewarded side) and for the expected number of errors. These were used
to estimate α_1 and α_2 from the data and yielded $\hat{\alpha}_1 = 0.910$ and $\hat{\alpha}_2 =
0.945$.

Bush analyzed these same data, using the beta model described by the
equations

$$P' = \begin{cases} \dfrac{\beta_1 P}{1 + (\beta_1 - 1)P}, & \text{if rewarded side is chosen,} \\[3ex] \dfrac{P}{\beta_2 + (1 - \beta_2)P}, & \text{if nonrewarded side is chosen.} \end{cases}$$

The estimation problem was more complex for the beta model than for
the alpha model because no explicit expressions are known for any of its
stochastic properties; therefore, the procedure is discussed a bit more fully.

An approximate graphical method was devised to get a first estimate of
the parameters. Choosing $\hat{P}_0 = 0.05$ (the direct estimate from the trial
49 data) and using the maximum likelihood equations (see Appendix 3)

which could not be solved explicitly, these rough estimates of β_1 and β_2 were adjusted numerically to make the errors in the equations small. The values so obtained were $\hat{P}_0 = 0.05$, $\hat{\beta}_1 = 1.05$, and $\hat{\beta}_2 = 0.70$. We note that the reward parameter β_1 is far less effective than the nonreward parameter β_2 in increasing the probability of choosing the rewarded side; whereas, with the alpha model, the reward operator is slightly more effective than the nonreward one.

Both models give adequate descriptions of the mean learning curve. To compare them further, values of certain run statistics were calculated. For the alpha model, expected values of these statistics can be calculated explicitly in terms of estimated parameters. For the beta model, no closed form of any property is known, so it was necessary to carry out Monte Carlo runs and to calculate the statistics from these, just as was done with the data. Twenty "stat-rats" were run.

If we let the random variable $x_{n,i}$ be defined as

$$x_{n,i} = \begin{cases} 1, & \text{if rat } i \text{ chooses the rewarded side on trial } n, \\ 0, & \text{if rat } i \text{ chooses the nonrewarded side on trial } n, \end{cases}$$

then the statistics examined were the mean number of runs of errors,

$$E(R) = \frac{1}{I} \sum_i \sum_n (1 - x_{n,i}) x_{n+1,i},$$

and the mean number of runs of errors of length j, which is denoted by $E(r_j)$.

The values of the corresponding statistics for the rats, their expected values for the two-commuting-operator alpha model, and the Monte Carlo values for the simple beta model are shown in Table 5. For three

TABLE 5. Comparison of Observed Statistics with Monte Carlo Values for the Beta Model and Expected Values for the Alpha Model

Statistic	Real Rats	Beta Model Stat-Rats	Two-Commuting-Operator Model
$E(R)$	6.60	6.15	6.67
$E(r_1)$	3.90	3.45	3.96
$E(r_2)$	1.30	1.15	1.11
$E(r_3)$	0.35	0.25	0.53
$E(r_4)$	0.40	0.50	0.33
$E(r_5)$	0.15	0.30	0.23
$\sum_{i=6}^{\infty} E(r_j)$	0.50	0.50	0.51

of these properties, the beta model figure is closer to the observed value than that of the alpha model, and for the other four this is reversed.

These results seem sufficiently encouraging to warrant further work on the beta model. The striking difference between the two models for these data is the fact that reward is more important than nonreward in the alpha model, whereas, the reverse is true for the beta model. This difference of interpretation can be utilized to design an experiment to discriminate between the two models. Such an experiment was designed and run; it is discussed in detail elsewhere (Galanter and Bush [1959] and Bush, Galanter, and Luce [1959]).

E. GAMMA MODEL

During discussions of this work at an S. S. R. C. Summer Institute (Stanford, 1957) several participants objected to the unboundedness of the v-scale in the beta model. Their feeling was that if v corresponds to response strength then it must be bounded. Michael D'Amato proposed that a linear operator of the form

$$v'(i) = \beta_i v(i) + \gamma_i$$

be assumed, since, with appropriate restrictions on β_i and γ_i, v would be bounded. As this suggestion seemed reasonable and interesting, questions arose whether it too could be given a plausible axiomatic justification and whether, as a learning operator, it seems to have sensible properties. Both points will be touched on.

As with the beta model, let us suppose that the positiveness, independence-of-unit, and independence-from-irrelevant-alternatives conditions are satisfied, but let us replace the unboundedness assumption by the following assumption.

Boundedness assumption.

For any fixed unit, the v-scale is bounded from above, i.e., there exists a value v_M such that $v \leq v_M$.

And let us add a condition that appears to have no empirical content but that is mathematically necessary.

Limiting condition.

$\lim_{v \to 0} f_i(v)$ *exists.*

These conditions imply that there are constants β_i and γ_i such that $f_i(v) = \beta_i v + \gamma_i v_m$. By the limiting condition, let $f_i(0) = \lim_{v \to 0} f_i(v)$. Of

course, by the independence-of-unit condition, we know that the numerical value of $f_i(0)$ depends upon the unit chosen; however, if we write it
as $f_i(0) = \gamma_i v_M$, where v_M is the bound specified in the boundedness
assumption, then γ_i is independent of the unit.   Clearly, $0 \leqq \gamma_i \leqq 1$.
Define $g_i(v) = f_i(v) - \gamma_i v_M$.   Since f_i satisfies the independence-of-unit
condition, so does g_i.   Thus $\beta_i = g_i(v_M)/v_M$ is independent of the unit.
Now, any $v \leqq v_M$ can be written $v = k v_M$, $k \leqq 1$, so by the independence-
of-unit condition on g_i we have

$$g_i(v) = g_i(k v_M)$$

$$= k g_i(v_M)$$

$$= \frac{v}{v_M} g_i(v_M)$$

$$= \beta_i v.$$

Thus

$$f_i(v) = g_i(v) + \gamma_i v_M$$

$$= \beta_i v + \gamma_i v_M.$$

If we choose our unit so that $v_M = 1$, as we may, then this can be written

$$f_i(v) = \beta_i v + \gamma_i.$$

This model has been dubbed the *gamma model*.

The positiveness condition, $f_i(v) > 0$ for $v > 0$, imposes obvious restrictions upon the parameters β_i and γ_i.

It should be observed that because of the additive constant γ_i it is not
possible to express P_T' simply as a function of P_T; thus, although path
independence is assumed for changes in the v-scale, it does not hold for the
probabilities in the gamma model.   This seems to be a strong point in
its favor; however, the considerations of the next section should be examined before a decision is reached.

It is clear that we might postulate operators of the general linear form
without any boundedness restriction on the v's, in which case the beta
model would be the specialization $\gamma_i = 0$ and the gamma model, the
specialization that v is bounded from above.   However, the more general
model does not always satisfy the basic independence-of-unit condition.

F. APPLICATION OF THE THREE MODELS TO A SPECIAL CASE

1. Introduction

By more or less plausible axiomatic defenses, we have been led to three
distinct classes of learning operators.   Clearly, at most one of them can

be correct, at least for a given situation.   The question, then, is whether some situation can be found in which two are so incorrect that a little mathematical manipulation will make their difficulties apparent.   Such a technique, when it can be applied, is quite powerful.   Of course, it is feasible only when there are not too many competing theories and when it is possible to specify in some detail a situation which, by itself, possesses a goodly amount of structure, since we must depend upon some structure beyond that contained in the learning models themselves to bring their failings to light.   We shall use the gambling structure of the last chapter, for which two of the three models exhibit peculiar properties, suggesting but by no means proving that the other model—the beta model—may be the most appropriate of the trio.   At the very least our results recommend fairly vigorous study of the beta model.

2. Partial Reinforcement

Consider an experiment in which the organism must select between two alternatives, of which one and only one will be rewarded on each trial. The alternative rewarded is determined by a chance event having probability π of occurring.   It has been customary to focus on the probability of the event, not on the event itself; however, as other aspects of the event may well be relevant, it seems sensible to describe the experiment in terms of the event.   So, let a and b be the two possible outcomes (e.g., a might mean "a pellet of food" and b that "nothing happens"), and let ρ denote the chance event, where $Pr(\rho) = \pi$; then $a\rho b$ denotes the first alternative and $a\bar{\rho}b$ the second.   The notation is the same as in section 3.B.1.   (A slight generalization is obtained by assuming alternatives $a\rho b$ and $a\sigma b$, where σ is not necessarily the complement of ρ.)   It is clear that such an experiment is a dynamic generalization of the static situation discussed in Chapter 3.

The event ρ chosen for the experiment is only one of a very wide class of events that might have been used, and the organism could have been placed in an experiment in which he had to discriminate relative likelihoods among these other events.   Thus $a\rho b$ and $a\bar{\rho}b$ are only two of many gambles that might have been used.   Let E denote some suitable set of events which includes ρ and $\bar{\rho}$, as well as some other events and their complements, and let G be the set of gambles of the form $a\sigma b$, where $\sigma \in E$.   Any particular trial of a learning experiment is similar to the static choice situation described in Chapter 3, and so we may make the same assumptions.   In particular, let us suppose that at each trial the following hold: axiom 1 for any subset of three gambles from G, the decomposition axiom 2, and the symmetry axiom 3.   In theorem 14 set $d = a$ and $c = b$.   Since a is interpreted as reward and b as nonreward, we may assume $P(a, b) = 1$. Furthermore, during the learning phase of the experiment it is safe to assume that $P(a\rho b, a\bar{\rho}b) \neq 0$ or 1. Then for *any* other $\sigma \in E$, such that $P(a\sigma b, a\rho b)$ and $P(a\sigma b, a\bar{\rho}b) \neq 0$ or 1, theorem 14 implies

$$v(a\rho b)v(a\bar{\rho}b) = v(a\sigma b)v(a\bar{\sigma}b).$$

Since the ρ's appear on one side and the σ's on the other side of this equation, we must conclude that

$$v(a\rho b)v(a\bar{\rho}b) = K,$$

where K is independent of the event.

Since this argument applies to each trial separately, there are two possibilities as we go from trial to trial: either K varies or it does not. The former possibility means that for every event σ not involved in the experiment, but not perfectly discriminated from either ρ or $\bar{\rho}$ of the experiment, $v(a\sigma b)$ and $v(a\bar{\sigma}b)$ are also undergoing systematic changes as a result of the learning taking place in the experiment. Similar phenomena, one class of which is known as stimulus generalization, have been observed, but no data now exist that would allow us to decide whether any generalization of the type just derived exists. Whether it really can be expected to occur for all events that are not perfectly discriminated with respect to likelihood from ρ and $\bar{\rho}$ seems questionable. Assuming not, we are led to investigate the assumption that K does not change with experience.

Now, for the first time in this argument we must introduce a specific learning model. We will proceed in this fashion: assume a model is correct, write the resulting expression for $v'(a\rho b)v'(a\bar{\rho}b) = K$ in terms of $v(a\rho b)$ and $v(a\bar{\rho}b)$ and then determine what this implies about behavior.

3. Alpha Model

For a specific choice-outcome event the alpha model is of the form

$$v'(a\rho b) = a_{11}v(a\rho b) + a_{12}v(a\bar{\rho}b)$$
$$v'(a\bar{\rho}b) = a_{21}v(a\rho b) + a_{22}v(a\bar{\rho}b),$$

where $a_{11} + a_{21} = a_{12} + a_{22}$. So,

$$v'(a\rho b)v'(a\bar{\rho}b) = K$$
$$= a_{11}a_{21}v(a\rho b)^2 + (a_{21}a_{12} + a_{11}a_{22})K + a_{12}a_{22}K^2/v(a\rho b)^2.$$

Rewriting,

$$a_{11}a_{21}v(a\rho b)^4 + (a_{21}a_{12} + a_{11}a_{22} - 1)Kv(a\rho b)^2 + a_{12}a_{22}K^2 = 0.$$

There are now two possibilities: either one of the coefficients of the first two terms is nonzero, or they are both zero. If the former, $v(a\rho b)$ can assume at most four different values, since it is determined by an equation of, at most, the fourth degree. But the value of $v(a\rho b)$ determines the value of $v(a\bar{\rho}b)$, so the choice probability for the two alternatives can assume at most four values different from 0 and 1. If the latter, we note that $K > 0$; hence the following equations hold:

$$a_{11}a_{21} = 0 \tag{2}$$

$$a_{12}a_{22} = 0 \tag{3}$$

$$a_{21}a_{12} + a_{11}a_{22} = 1 \tag{4}$$

$$a_{11} + a_{21} = a_{12} + a_{22}. \tag{5}$$

If $a_{11} = 0$, then, by equation 4, $a_{21}a_{12} = 1$, and so $a_{12} \neq 0$. Thus, by equation 3, $a_{22} = 0$. Substituting in equation 5, $a_{21} = a_{12}$, so from $a_{21}a_{12} = 1$ we conclude $a_{12} = a_{21} = 1$. In a similar fashion, if $a_{21} = 0$, then $a_{12} = 0$ and $a_{11} = a_{22} = 1$. In the second of these two cases the learning model reduces to

$$v'(a\rho b) = v(a\rho b) \quad \text{and} \quad v'(a\bar{\rho}b) = v(a\bar{\rho}b),$$

and there is no learning. In the first it becomes

$$v'(a\rho b) = v(a\bar{\rho}b) \quad \text{and} \quad v'(a\bar{\rho}b) = v(a\rho b),$$

and the choice probability simply oscillates between two values; again there is no learning.

4. Beta Model

For a specific choice-outcome event, the beta model is of the form

$$v'(a\rho b) = \beta_1 v(a\rho b)$$
$$v'(a\bar{\rho}b) = \beta_2 v(a\bar{\rho}b).$$

So,

$$v'(a\rho b)v'(a\bar{\rho}b) = K$$
$$= \beta_1\beta_2 v(a\rho b)v(a\bar{\rho}b)$$
$$= \beta_1\beta_2 K.$$

Since $K > 0$, $\beta_1\beta_2 = 1$. This is easily seen to imply the simple beta model with $\beta = (\beta_1)^2$.

5. Gamma Model

For a specific choice-outcome event, the gamma model is of the form

$$v'(a\rho b) = \beta_1 v(a\rho b) + \gamma_1$$
$$v'(a\bar{\rho}b) = \beta_2 v(a\bar{\rho}b) + \gamma_2.$$

So,

$$v'(a\rho b)v'(a\bar{\rho}b) = K$$
$$= K\beta_1\beta_2 + \beta_1\gamma_2 v(a\rho b) + \gamma_1\beta_2 K/v(a\rho b) + \gamma_1\gamma_2.$$

Rewriting,

$$v(a\rho b)^2 A + v(a\rho b)B + C = 0,$$

where $A = \beta_1\gamma_2$

$$B = (\beta_1\beta_2 - 1)K + \gamma_1\gamma_2$$

$$C = \gamma_1\beta_2 K.$$

As with the alpha model, there are two possibilities: either some of the coefficients of the quadratic equation are non-zero, in which case $v(a\rho b)$ can have at most two values, or $A = B = C = 0$. If the first possibility obtains, then the probability of choosing alternative $a\rho b$ instead of $a\bar{\rho}b$ can have, at most, two values other than 0 or 1. The second possibility requires more detailed analysis. Suppose that $\beta_1 = 0$, then $B = 0 = -K + \gamma_1\gamma_2$. Since $K > 0$, it follows that both $\gamma_1 \neq 0$ and $\gamma_2 \neq 0$. But that coupled with $C = 0$ implies $\beta_2 = 0$. Similarly, if $\beta_2 = 0$, then $\beta_1 = 0$. Going back to the learning operators, we see that this implies $v(a\rho b) = \gamma_1$ and $v(a\bar{\rho}b) = \gamma_2$ on all trials, which means no learning. Alternatively, we may suppose that $\beta_1 \neq 0$ and $\beta_2 \neq 0$. It follows immediately from $A = C = 0$ that $\gamma_1 = \gamma_2 = 0$. This with $B = 0$ implies that $\beta_1 = 1/\beta_2$, which is the beta model just discussed.

6. Conclusions

In summary, then, we have shown the following. If the axioms of Chapter 3 (actually, only axioms 1, 2, and 3) hold at each trial of a two-choice experiment, then either

(1) events outside the experiment, but not perfectly discriminated according to relative likelihood from the one in the experiment, must exhibit systematic changes paralleling the learning in the experiment (a type of stimulus generalization); or

(2) $v(a\rho b)v(a\bar{\rho}b)$ must have the same value on all trials.

Case 2 implies different things, depending upon which learning model is assumed. For the alpha model, either there is no learning or the choice probability has, at most, four values different from 0 and 1. For the beta model, a minor restriction results, which, however, has no implications for the choice probabilities. For the gamma model, either the choice probability has, at most, two values different from 0 and 1, or it is actually the simple beta model.

What, then, may we conclude? This is not easy to say, since the argument is based on a number of assumptions, but it appears to give some additional support to the beta model. Nonetheless, there are other possibilities. First, one or more of the axioms from Chapter 3 may not hold on each trial of a learning experiment. These are strong assumptions, as we have seen earlier, and it may well be that they are badly violated during learning. Second, perhaps the generalization phenomenon described above does exist, although, as previously indicated, it is doubtful, since the mathematics requires an amount of generalization that seems to exceed anything that has been observed. Third, perhaps behavioral probabilities really can have only a few values. Of the three, this seems to be the most inviting alternative, and so it bears a little more comment.

It is clear that such discreteness of behavior is distinct from that derived in theorem 13, although, once again, it does indicate that assuming axioms 1 and 2 is only just short of assuming discreteness. The question at hand is whether such behavior is exhibited in learning experiments. Our immediate No reaction must be tempered by the realization that almost without exception learning data are presented as summary statistics for several organisms. Thus we cannot expect to see any obvious signs of discreteness in the learning curve, even if it exists for each organism separately. Furthermore, data for single organisms will not show it very clearly either, since it is extraordinarily difficult to decide whether a sequence of binary responses arose from a gradually changing probability or from sudden jumps among three or four discrete probabilities. To reject conclusively the possibility that discrete choice probabilities exist, a delicate and systematic empirical search will be required.

G. SOME ASYMPTOTIC PROPERTIES OF THE BETA MODEL

1. Introduction

Although closed forms, or even computable expressions, which could be used to estimate parameters have not yet been obtained for any properties of the beta model, some information can be gained about its asymptotic behavior. Such results are not without interest, since Estes has focused considerable attention upon the limiting behavior of the alpha model, and comparisons have been made between these predictions and the behavior of subjects at the end of several hundred trials. The results to be presented are unfortunately very incomplete, but they do give some hint about the asymptotic behavior of the beta model. There seems to be every indication that the dependence upon parameter values is quite complicated.

Only experiments in which there are two alternatives and two outcomes are discussed. Once the organism chooses one of the alternatives, the outcome is assumed to be determined by a chance event whose probability is fixed by the experimenter, a different probability being used for each alternative. Suppose we denote by 1 and 2 the two alternatives and by P_n, the probability that alternative 1 is chosen on trial n. Assuming that axiom 1 holds on each trial, then theorem 3 implies

$$P_n = \frac{v_n(1)}{v_n(1) + v_n(2)}$$

$$= \frac{v_n}{v_n + 1},\tag{6}$$

where $v_n = v_n(1)/v_n(2)$.

The symbols 1 and 2 are also used to denote the outcomes, and let E_{ij}, $i,j = 1,2$, denote the event that choice i is made and outcome j occurs. The four transition equations of the simple beta model may then be written as

$$v_{n+1} = \left\{ \begin{matrix} \beta_{11}v_n \\ \beta_{12}v_n \\ \dfrac{1}{\beta_{21}} v_n \\ \dfrac{1}{\beta_{22}} v_n \end{matrix} \right\} \text{ if } \left\{ \begin{matrix} E_{11} \\ E_{12} \\ E_{21} \\ E_{22} \end{matrix} \right\} \begin{matrix} \text{occurs, which it does} \\ \text{with probability} \end{matrix} \left\{ \begin{matrix} P_n\pi_1 \\ P_n(1 - \pi_1) \\ (1 - P_n)\pi_2 \\ (1 - P_n)(1 - \pi_2) \end{matrix} \right\},\tag{7}$$

where π_i is the probability that outcome 1 occurs, given that alternative i has been chosen.

Given any real number k, the expectation of v_{n+1}^k conditional on v_n is given by

$$E(v_{n+1}^k|v_n) = P_n\pi_1\beta_{11}^k v_n^k + P_n(1 - \pi_1)\beta_{12}^k v_n^k + (1 - P_n)\pi_2 \left(\frac{v_n}{\beta_{21}}\right)^k$$

$$+ (1 - P_n)(1 - \pi_2)\left(\frac{v_n}{\beta_{22}}\right)^k$$

$$= [A(k) - B(k)]P_n v_n^k + B(k)v_n^k,\tag{8}$$

where

$$A(k) = \pi_1 \beta_{11}^k + (1 - \pi_1)\beta_{12}^k$$

$$B(k) = \frac{\pi_2}{\beta_{21}^k} + \frac{(1 - \pi_2)}{\beta_{22}^k}. \tag{9}$$

Taking expectations over v_n in equation 8,

$$E(v_{n+1}^k) = [A(k) - B(k)]E(P_n v_n^k) + B(k)E(v_n^k). \tag{10}$$

This is the first of three equations that are to be used to obtain results on the limiting behavior of $E(P_n)$. The second is simply equation 6 slightly rewritten:

$$P_n v_n = v_n - P_n. \tag{11}$$

The third we now derive.

By taking logarithms in equation 7, we obtain

$$\log v_{n+1} - \log v_n = \left\{ \begin{array}{l} \log \beta_{11} \\ \log \beta_{12} \\ -\log \beta_{21} \\ -\log \beta_{22} \end{array} \right\} \text{with} \atop \text{probability} \left\{ \begin{array}{l} P_n \pi_1 \\ P_n(1 - \pi_1) \\ (1 - P_n)\pi_2 \\ (1 - P_n)(1 - \pi_2) \end{array} \right\} \tag{12}$$

Thus the expectation of $\log v_{n+1} - \log v_n$, holding v_n fixed, is

$$E(\log v_{n+1}|v_n) - \log v_n = P_n \pi_1 \log \beta_{11} + P_n(1 - \pi_1) \log \beta_{12}$$
$$- (1 - P_n)\pi_2 \log \beta_{21}$$
$$- (1 - P_n)(1 - \pi_2) \log \beta_{22}$$
$$= P_n\{(\log \beta_{11})[\pi_1(\sigma_1 + 1) - \sigma_1]$$
$$+ (\log \beta_{21})[\pi_2(\sigma_2 + 1) - \sigma_2]\}$$
$$- (\log \beta_{21})[\pi_2(\sigma_2 + 1) - \sigma_2], \tag{13}$$

where we have defined σ_i by the equation

$$(\beta_{i1})^{\sigma_i} = 1/\beta_{i2}. \tag{14}$$

These new parameters are easy to interpret: σ_i tells the number of times that event E_{i1} must occur to undo one occurence of event E_{i2}.

Define the quantity

$$P^* = \frac{\pi_2(\sigma_2 + 1) - \sigma_2}{\frac{\log \beta_{11}}{\log \beta_{21}}[\pi_1(\sigma_1 + 1) - \sigma_1] + [\pi_2(\sigma_2 + 1) - \sigma_2]}. \tag{15}$$

Introducing this notation in equation 13 and taking expectations over v_n yields

$$E(\log v_{n+1}) - E(\log v_n) = \{(\log \beta_{11})[\pi_1(\sigma_1 + 1) - \sigma_1] \\ + (\log \beta_{21})[\pi_2(\sigma_2 + 1) - \sigma_2]\}[E(P_n) - P^*]. \quad (16)$$

This is the third basic equation.

In what follows these three equations are used to find out certain things about the limit of $E(P_n)$ as $n \to \infty$. The results are not complete, and they are rather difficult to summarize in a compact form. In the next section we show that if $\lim_{n\to\infty} E(v_n)$ and $\lim_{n\to\infty} E(1/v_n)$ both exist (including ∞ as a possible value) and if they do not both equal ∞ then $\lim_{n\to\infty} E(P_n)$ exists. Furthermore, its value is determined if either $\lim_{n\to\infty} E(v_n)$ or $\lim_{n\to\infty} E(1/v_n)$ is 0 or if both are finite but different from 0.

Having partially reduced the problem to the limiting behavior of $E(v_n)$ and $E(1/v_n)$, the third section presents some conditions sufficient to ensure the existence of these limits. Again, only partial results are obtained. Unfortunately, the important cases in which the limits are finite, but nonzero, are least well understood.

In the fourth section this complex of results is applied to an important special case.

2. Relations Among Asymptotic Expectations

Theorem 15. *Let k be an integer ≥ 1.*

(i) *If $\lim_{n\to\infty} E(v_n^i)$ exists and is finite, $i = 1, 2, \cdots, k$, and if $A(i) \neq B(i)$ and $A(i) \neq 1$, then $\lim_{n\to\infty} E(P_n)$ exists and*

$$\lim_{n\to\infty} E(v_n^k) = \left[\frac{A(k) - B(k)}{A(k) - 1}\right] \prod_{i=0}^{k-1} \left[\frac{1 - B(i)}{A(i) - 1}\right] \lim_{n\to\infty} E(P_n),$$

where

$$\frac{1 - B(0)}{A(0) - 1} = 1.$$

(ii) *If $\lim_{n\to\infty} E(1/v_n^i)$ exists and is finite, $i = 1, 2, \cdots, k$, and if $B(-i) \neq A(-i)$ and $B(-i) \neq 1$, then $\lim_{n\to\infty} E(P_n)$ exists and*

$$\lim_{n\to\infty} E(1/v_n^k) = \left[\frac{A(-k) - B(-k)}{1 - B(-k)}\right] \prod_{i=0}^{k-1} \left[\frac{1 - A(-i)}{1 - B(-i)}\right] [1 - \lim_{n\to\infty} E(P_n)],$$

where

$$\frac{1 - A(0)}{1 - B(0)} = 1.$$

PROOF. From equation 11,

$$E(P_n v_n^i) = E(v_n^i) - E(P_n v_n^{i-1}).$$

Substituting in equation 10,

$$E(v_{n+1}^i) - E(v_n^i) = [A(i) - 1]E(v_n^i) - [A(i) - B(i)]E(P_n v_n^{i-1}).$$

For $i \le k$, take limits as $n \to \infty$. Since $\lim\limits_{n \to \infty} E(v_n^i)$ exists and is finite, the left side becomes 0, and so

$$\lim_{n \to \infty} E(v_n^i) = \left[\frac{A(i) - B(i)}{A(i) - 1}\right] \lim_{n \to \infty} E(P_n v_n^{i-1}). \tag{17}$$

If $k = 1$, then the result is proved. For larger k we prove it by induction. By equation 10 and the fact that $A(i) \ne B(i)$,

$$E(P_n v_n^{k-1}) = \frac{E(v_{n+1}^{k-1}) - B(k - 1)E(v_n^{k-1})}{A(k - 1) - B(k - 1)}.$$

Take limits and substitute in equation 17 with $i = k$:

$$\lim_{n \to \infty} E(v_n^k) = \left[\frac{A(k) - B(k)}{A(k) - 1}\right]\left[\frac{1 - B(k - 1)}{A(k - 1) - B(k - 1)}\right] \lim_{n \to \infty} E(v_n^{k-1}).$$

Substituting the induction hypothesis yields the first part of the assertion. The second part is proved in a similar manner.

Corollary. *If $\lim\limits_{n \to \infty} E(v_n)$ exists and is finite and $A(1) \ne B(1)$ or if $\lim\limits_{n \to \infty} E(1/v_n)$ exists and is finite and $B(-1) \ne A(-1)$, then $\lim\limits_{n \to \infty} E(P_n)$ exists.*

PROOF. This follows from the theorem, noting, however, that $A(1)$ may equal 1 in equation 17 and $B(-1)$ may equal 1 in the analogue of equation 17.

Theorem 16.

(i) *Suppose $\lim\limits_{n \to \infty} E(v_n)$ exists and is finite. If $\lim\limits_{n \to \infty} E(v_n) = 0$, then $\lim\limits_{n \to \infty} E(P_n) = 0$ and $\lim\limits_{n \to \infty} E(1/v_n) = \infty$. If $\lim\limits_{n \to \infty} E(P_n) = 0$ and $A(1) \ne 1$, then $\lim\limits_{n \to \infty} E(v_n) = 0$.*

(ii) *Suppose* $\lim_{n\to\infty} E(1/v_n)$ *exists and is finite. If* $\lim_{n\to\infty} E(1/v_n) = 0$, *then* $\lim_{n\to\infty} E(P_n) = 1$ *and* $\lim_{n\to\infty} E(v_n) = \infty$. *If* $\lim_{n\to\infty} E(P_n) = 1$ *and* $B(-1) \neq 1$, *then* $\lim_{n\to\infty} E(1/v_n) = 0$.

PROOF.   Only part i will be proved, since the other part is similar. It follows directly from equation 11 that

$$0 \leqq E(P_n) = E(v_n) - E(P_n v_n) \leqq E(v_n),$$

and so if $\lim_{n\to\infty} E(v_n) = 0$ then $\lim_{n\to\infty} E(P_n)$ exists and equals 0.

We next show that $\lim_{n\to\infty} E(1/v_n) = \infty$. By definition of the limit, for each $\epsilon > 0$ there exists an $N(\epsilon)$ such that for any $n > N(\epsilon)$, $\epsilon > E(v_n)$. Let ϕ_n denote the distribution of v_n on trial n and let k be any number > 1; then

$$\epsilon > E(v_n)$$
$$= \int_0^{k\epsilon} x\phi_n(x)\,dx + \int_{k\epsilon}^{\infty} x\phi_n(x)\,dx$$
$$> 0 + k\epsilon \int_{k\epsilon}^{\infty} \phi_n(x)\,dx.$$

Hence, $\int_0^{k\epsilon} \phi_n(x)\,dx > 1 - 1/k$. Using this, we obtain

$$E(1/v_n) = \int_0^{k\epsilon} \frac{\phi_n(x)}{x}\,dx + \int_{k\epsilon}^{\infty} \frac{\phi_n(x)}{x}\,dx$$
$$> \frac{1}{k\epsilon} \int_0^{k\epsilon} \phi_n(x)\,dx + 0$$
$$> \frac{k-1}{k^2\epsilon}.$$

But $k > 1$, so as $\epsilon \to 0$, $E(1/v_n) \to \infty$.

If $\lim_{n\to\infty} E(P_n) = 0$ and $A(1) \neq 1$, then by equation 17, $\lim_{n\to\infty} E(v_n) = 0$.

Theorem 17.   *If* $\lim_{n\to\infty} E(P_n)$ *exists and if* $(\log \beta_{11})[\pi_1(\sigma_1 + 1) - \sigma_1] + (\log \beta_{21})[\pi_2(\sigma_2 + 1) - \sigma_2] \neq 0$, *then either* $\lim_{n\to\infty} E(P_n) = P^*$, *where* P^* *is defined by equation 15*, $\lim_{n\to\infty} E(v_n) = \infty$, *or* $\lim_{n\to\infty} E(1/v_n) = \infty$.

PROOF.   Since $\lim_{n\to\infty} E(P_n)$ exists, we know from equation 16 that $\lim_{n\to\infty} [E(\log v_{n+1}) - E(\log v_n)]$ exists; let its value be denoted by K. It is well known (see, for example, Hardy [1946], p. 168) that this implies that $E(\log v_n)/n$ approaches K as $n \to \infty$, so if $K \neq 0$, $E(\log v_n)$ is not bounded as $n \to \infty$. However, since $-E(1/v_n) \leqq E(\log v_n) \leqq E(v_n)$, it follows that either $\lim_{n \to \infty} E(1/v_n) = \infty$ or $\lim_{n \to \infty} E(v_n) = \infty$. If, however, $K = 0$, then since $(\log \beta_{11})[\pi_1(\sigma_1 + 1) - \sigma] + (\log \beta_{21})[\pi_2(\sigma_2 + 1) - \sigma_2] \neq 0$ we conclude from equation 16 that $\lim_{n \to \infty} E(P_n) = P^*$.

Corollary. *If* $\lim_{n \to \infty} E(v_n)$ *and* $\lim_{n \to \infty} E(1/v_n)$ *both exist and are finite, if* $A(1) \neq B(1)$ *or* $B(-1) \neq A(-1)$, *and if* $(\log \beta_{11})[\pi_1(\sigma_1 + 1) - \sigma_1] + (\log \beta_{21})[\pi_2(\sigma_2 + 1) - \sigma_2] \neq 0$, *then* $\lim_{n \to \infty} E(P_n) = P^*$.

PROOF. By the corollary to theorem 15, the hypotheses imply that $\lim_{n \to \infty} E(P_n)$ exists, and by this theorem it must equal P^*.

3. Existence and Values of $\lim_{n \to \infty} \mathbf{E(v}_n)$ and $\lim_{n \to \infty} \mathbf{E(1/v}_n)$

It is apparent from the results just obtained that the behavior of $\lim_{n \to \infty} E(P_n)$, which is what interests us, depends at least in some cases upon the behavior of $\lim_{n \to \infty} E(v_n)$ and $\lim_{n \to \infty} E(1/v_n)$. For example, aside from the question of what happens when $A(i) = B(i)$, $i = 1, -1$, it is completely determined when they are both finite or when one is zero; however, we do not know what happens when one is finite (but not zero) and the other is infinite or when both are infinite. We now want to see what can be said about these two limits.

Theorem 18.

(i) *If* $A(1)$, $B(1) > 1$, *then* $\lim_{n \to \infty} E(v_n) = \infty$. *If* $A(1)$, $B(1) < 1$, *then* $\lim_{n \to \infty} E(v_n) = 0$. *If* $\lim_{n \to \infty} E(v_n) = \infty$, *then* $A(1) \geqq 1$.

(ii) *If* $A(-1)$, $B(-1) > 1$, *then* $\lim_{n \to \infty} E(1/v_n) = \infty$. *If* $A(-1)$, $B(-1) < 1$, *then* $\lim_{n \to \infty} E(1/v_n) = 0$. *If* $\lim_{n \to \infty} E(1/v_n) = \infty$, *then* $B(-1) \geqq 1$.

PROOF. As in the preceding theorems, only part i will be proved, since the other part is similar.

By equation 11, we know $E(P_n v_n) < E(v_n)$. Substitute this into equation 10 with $k = 1$,

$$E(v_{n+1}) = E(P_n v_n)[A(1) - B(1)] + B(1)E(v_n)$$
$$\lesseqqgtr A(1)E(v_n),$$

according as $A(1) \gtreqqless B(1)$. By induction, $E(v_n) \lesseqqgtr A(1)^n E(v_0)$. Thus,

if $1 < A(1) \lessgtr B(1)$, $\lim\limits_{n \to \infty} E(v_n) = \infty$, and, if $1 > A(1) \gtrless B(1)$, $\lim\limits_{n \to \infty} E(v_n)$
$= 0$.

Similarly, $E(P_n) < E(v_n)$ from equation 11, so from equation 10 we have

$$E(v_{n+1}) = [E(v_n) - E(P_n)][A(1) - B(1)] + B(1)E(v_n)$$
$$= A(1)E(v_n) + [B(1) - A(1)]E(P_n)$$
$$\lessgtr B(1)E(v_n),$$

according as $A(1) \lessgtr B(1)$. By induction, $E(v_n) \lessgtr B(1)^n E(v_0)$. Thus, if $1 < B(1) \lessgtr A(1)$, $\lim\limits_{n \to \infty} E(v_n) = \infty$, and, if $1 > B(1) \gtrless A(1)$, $\lim\limits_{n \to \infty} E(v_n)$
$= 0$.

Now, suppose $\lim\limits_{n \to \infty} E(v_n) = \infty$, which means, by definition, that for every $M > 0$ there exists an N such that for every $n > N$, $E(v_n) > M$. From equations 10 and 11

$$E(v_{n+1}) - E(v_n) = [A(1) - 1]E(v_n) - E(P_n)[A(1) - B(1)].$$

If $A(1) < 1$, then it is clear that we can choose M sufficiently large that for all x, $0 \leqq x \leqq 1$,

$$[A(1) - 1]M - x[A(1) - B(1)] < 0.$$

But this means that, for some N, $E(v_n) > M$ for all $n > N$ and that $E(v_{n+1}) < E(v_n)$. This implies $\lim\limits_{n \to \infty} E(v_n)$ is finite, contrary to assumption. So, $A(1) \geqq 1$.

It is evident that the relations between the $A(i)$, $B(i)$, and 1 are important in determining the asymptotic behavior of the beta model, so it is worth while stating these explicitly in terms of the original parameters:

$$A(1) \geqq 1 \quad \text{if and only if} \quad \pi_1 \gtreqless \frac{1 - \beta_{12}}{\beta_{11} - \beta_{12}}$$

$$B(1) \geqq 1 \quad \text{if and only if} \quad \pi_2 \lesseqgtr \frac{\beta_{21}(1 - \beta_{22})}{\beta_{21} - \beta_{22}}$$

$$A(-1) \geqq 1 \quad \text{if and only if} \quad \pi_1 \lesseqgtr \frac{\beta_{11}(1 - \beta_{12})}{\beta_{11} - \beta_{12}} \tag{18}$$

$$B(-1) \geqq 1 \quad \text{if and only if} \quad \pi_2 \gtreqless \frac{1 - \beta_{22}}{\beta_{21} - \beta_{22}}$$

These are trivial consequences of equation 9.

Another set of constraints arises when $\lim\limits_{n\to\infty} E(v_n)$ and $\lim\limits_{n\to\infty} E(1/v_n)$ are both finite and nonzero, for then we know that $\lim\limits_{n\to\infty} E(P_n) = P^*$ must lie between 0 and 1.   If we suppose that β_{1j} and β_{2j} are both greater than 1 (as we would expect if outcome j denotes reward) or both less than 1 (as we would expect if outcome j denotes nonreward), then it is easy to show from equation 15 that either $\pi_i > \sigma_i/(\sigma_i + 1)$, $i = 1, 2$, or $\pi_i < \sigma_i/(\sigma_i + 1)$, $i = 1, 2$.

The next question, then, is whether the quantity $\sigma_i/(\sigma_i + 1)$ has any simple relation to the quantities $(1 - \beta_{i2})/(\beta_{i1} - \beta_{i2})$ and $\beta_{i1}(1 - \beta_{i2})/(\beta_{i1} - \beta_{i2})$ that arise above.   We first prove

Lemma 12.   *If $x, y > 1$, then*

$$\frac{\log x}{x - 1} < \frac{y}{y - 1} \log y.$$

PROOF.   Observe that, for $x > 1$, $(\log x)/(x - 1)$ is monotonically decreasing, so

$$\frac{\log x}{x - 1} < \lim_{z \to 1} \frac{\log z}{z - 1}$$

$$= \lim_{z \to 1} \frac{1/z}{1}$$

$$= 1.$$

For $y > 1$, $(y \log y)/(y - 1)$ is monotonically increasing, so

$$\frac{y}{y - 1} \log y > \lim_{z \to 1} \frac{z}{z - 1} \log z$$

$$= \lim_{z \to 1} \frac{1 + \log z}{1}$$

$$= 1,$$

which proves the result.

Theorem 19.   *If $\beta_{i1} > 1 > \beta_{i2}$, then*

$$\frac{\beta_{i1}(1 - \beta_{i2})}{\beta_{i1} - \beta_{i2}} > \frac{\sigma_i}{\sigma_i + 1} > \frac{1 - \beta_{i2}}{\beta_{i1} - \beta_{i2}}.$$

PROOF.   Let $x = 1/\beta_{i2}$ and $y = \beta_{i1}$ in the lemma:

$$\frac{\log\,(1/\beta_{i2})}{(1/\beta_{i2}) - 1} < \frac{\beta_{i1}\,\log\,\beta_{i1}}{\beta_{i1} - 1}.$$

Since $\beta_{i1} > 1$, $\log\,\beta_{i1} > 0$, and since $\beta_{i2} < 1$, $(1/\beta_{i2}) - 1 > 0$. Thus, we may rewrite the inequality as

$$\sigma_i = \frac{\log\,(1/\beta_{i2})}{\log\,\beta_{i1}} < \frac{\beta_{i1}(1 - \beta_{i2})}{\beta_{i2}(\beta_{i1} - 1)},$$

where σ_i has been introduced via equation 14. Let $C = \beta_{i1}(1 - \beta_{i2})/(\beta_{i1} - \beta_{i2})$. Since $\beta_{i1} > 1$, $C < 1$. Observe that

$$\frac{C}{1 - C} = \frac{\beta_{i1}(1 - \beta_{i2})}{\beta_{i2}(\beta_{i1} - 1)},$$

so $\sigma_i < C/(1 - C)$, which with $C < 1$ implies $\sigma_i/(\sigma_i + 1) < C$. This establishes half of the inequality; the other half is proved similarly by letting $x = \beta_{i1}$ and $y = 1/\beta_{i2}$ in the lemma.

4. A Special Case

To gain insight into what is and is not known about the asymptotic behavior of the beta model, it is useful to examine a special case of some inherent interest, namely:

$$\beta_{11} = \beta_{21} = \beta_1 > 1$$
$$\beta_{12} = \beta_{22} = \beta_2 < 1 \tag{19}$$
$$\pi_1 = \pi, \qquad \pi_2 = 1 - \pi.$$

It follows immediately that
$$\sigma_1 = \sigma_2 = \sigma. \tag{20}$$

We will now develop a number of simple relations that hold among the parameters for this special case. They will then be used to isolate four inherently different asymptotic conditions.

Define

$$\delta_1 = \frac{\beta_1 - 1}{\beta_1 - \beta_2} \quad \text{and} \quad \delta_2 = \frac{1 - \beta_2}{\beta_1 - \beta_2}. \tag{21}$$

As is easily seen, equation 18 reduces to

$$A(1) \gtrless 1 \quad \text{if and only if} \quad \pi \gtrless \delta_2$$

$$B(1) \gtrless 1 \quad \text{if and only if} \quad \pi \gtrless \beta_2\delta_1$$

$$A(-1) \gtrless 1 \quad \text{if and only if} \quad \pi \lessgtr \beta_1\delta_2 \tag{22}$$

$$B(-1) \gtrless 1 \quad \text{if and only if} \quad \pi \lessgtr \delta_1.$$

From equation 9, we can show that

$$A(1) \gtrless B(1) \quad \text{if and only if} \quad \sigma \lessgtr 1$$

$$A(-1) \gtrless B(-1) \quad \text{if and only if} \quad \sigma \gtrless 1. \tag{23}$$

We prove only the former: $A(1) \gtrless B(1)$ is, by definition, equivalent to

$$\pi\beta_1 + (1 - \pi)\beta_2 \gtrless \frac{(1 - \pi)}{\beta_1} + \frac{\pi}{\beta_2}.$$

So

$$\pi\left(\beta_1 - \frac{1}{\beta_2}\right) \gtrless (1 - \pi)\left(\frac{1}{\beta_1} - \beta_2\right),$$

i.e.,

$$\frac{\pi}{\beta_2}(\beta_1\beta_2 - 1) \gtrless -\frac{(1 - \pi)}{\beta_1}(\beta_1\beta_2 - 1).$$

Since $\pi/\beta_2 > 0$ and $-(1 - \pi)/\beta_1 < 0$, this is equivalent to $\beta_1\beta_2 - 1 \gtrless 0$, which in turn is equivalent to $\sigma \lessgtr 1$.

From equation 22 and the assumption (equation 19) that $\beta_1 > 1 > \beta_2$, it follows that

$$A(1) < 1 \quad \text{implies} \quad A(-1) > 1$$

$$A(-1) < 1 \quad \text{implies} \quad A(1) > 1$$

$$B(1) < 1 \quad \text{implies} \quad B(-1) > 1 \tag{24}$$

$$B(-1) < 1 \quad \text{implies} \quad B(1) > 1.$$

We show only the first: if $A(1) < 1$, then, by equation 22, $\pi < \delta_2$; however, $\beta_1 > 1$ means $\delta_2 < \beta_1\delta_2$, so $\pi < \beta_1\delta_2$; whence, by equation 22, $A(-1) > 1$. The other three proofs are similar.

Next, we observe that

$$A(1) + B(-1) = \beta_1 + \beta_2$$

$$A(-1) + B(1) = \frac{1}{\beta_1} + \frac{1}{\beta_2}. \tag{25}$$

It follows immediately from equation 25 that

$$\beta_1 + \beta_2 \gtrless 2 \quad \text{and} \quad A(1) \lessgtr 1 \quad \text{imply} \quad B(-1) \gtrless 1$$

$$\beta_1 + \beta_2 \gtrless 2 \quad \text{and} \quad B(-1) \lessgtr 1 \quad \text{imply} \quad A(1) \gtrless 1$$

$$\frac{1}{\beta_1} + \frac{1}{\beta_2} \gtrless 2 \quad \text{and} \quad A(-1) \lessgtr 1 \quad \text{imply} \quad B(1) \gtrless 1 \qquad (26)$$

$$\frac{1}{\beta_1} + \frac{1}{\beta_2} \gtrless 2 \quad \text{and} \quad B(1) \lessgtr 1 \quad \text{imply} \quad A(-1) \gtrless 1.$$

We show that

$$\beta_1 + \beta_2 < 2 \quad \text{and} \quad \frac{1}{\beta_1} + \frac{1}{\beta_2} < 2 \quad \text{are impossible}$$

$$\beta_1 + \beta_2 > 2 \quad \text{and} \quad \frac{1}{\beta_1} + \frac{1}{\beta_2} < 2 \quad \text{imply} \quad \sigma < 1 \qquad (27)$$

$$\beta_1 + \beta_2 < 2 \quad \text{and} \quad \frac{1}{\beta_1} + \frac{1}{\beta_2} > 2 \quad \text{imply} \quad \sigma > 1.$$

First, if $\beta_1 + \beta_2 < 2$, then $1/\beta_1 > 1/(2 - \beta_2)$, and so $2 > (1/\beta_1) + (1/\beta_2) > [1/(2 - \beta_2)] + (1/\beta_2)$. Cross multiplying and simplifying yields $(\beta_2 - 1)^2 < 0$, which is impossible. Second, $(1/\beta_1) + (1/\beta_2) < 2$ implies $2\beta_1\beta_2 > \beta_1 + \beta_2 > 2$, and so $\beta_1 > 1/\beta_2$, i.e., $\sigma < 1$. The third proof is similar to the second.

Finally, it follows immediately from the definitions in equation 21 that

$$\beta_2\delta_1 \gtrless \delta_2 \quad \text{if and only if} \quad \sigma \lessgtr 1$$

$$\beta_1\delta_2 \gtrless \delta_1 \quad \text{if and only if} \quad \sigma \gtrless 1$$

$$\delta_1 \gtrless \delta_2 \quad \text{if and only if} \quad \beta_1 + \beta_2 \gtrless 2 \qquad (28)$$

$$\beta_1\delta_2 \gtrless \beta_2\delta_1 \quad \text{if and only if} \quad (1/\beta_1) + (1/\beta_2) \gtrless 2.$$

We now have sufficient knowledge about the interrelations among the parameters to see what can happen. From equation 27 we note that there are four different conditions definable in terms of the organism parameters β_1 and β_2:

	$\beta_1 + \beta_2$	$\dfrac{1}{\beta_1} + \dfrac{1}{\beta_2}$	σ
I	<2	>2	>1
II	>2	<2	<1
III	>2	>2	>1
IV	>2	>2	<1

$$(29)$$

Each of these must be analyzed separately, but as they are all similar only condition I is worked out in detail. Since $\sigma > 1$, equation 23 implies $A(1) < B(1)$ and $A(-1) > B(-1)$, so considering where the 1's may be located there are nine possibilities (ignoring equalities):

1. $A(1) < B(1) < 1,$ $A(-1) > B(-1) > 1$
2. $A(1) < B(1) < 1,$ $A(-1) > 1 > B(-1)$
3. $A(1) < B(1) < 1,$ $1 > A(-1) > B(-1)$
4. $A(1) < 1 < B(1),$ $A(-1) > B(-1) > 1$
5. $A(1) < 1 < B(1),$ $A(-1) > 1 > B(-1)$
6. $A(1) < 1 < B(1),$ $1 > A(-1) > B(-1)$
7. $1 < A(1) < B(1),$ $A(-1) > B(-1) > 1$
8. $1 < A(1) < B(1),$ $A(-1) > 1 > B(-1)$
9. $1 < A(1) < B(1),$ $1 > A(-1) > B(-1).$

According to equation 24, $B(-1) < 1$ implies $B(1) > 1$, so case 2 cannot occur. Also by equation 24, $A(1) < 1$ implies $A(-1) > 1$, so both cases 3 and 6 are impossible. Finally, by equation 26, $A(1) > 1$ implies $B(-1) < 1$, so case 7 cannot occur. This leaves five cases: 1, 4, 5, 8, and 9. From the definition of condition I, equation 28, and the fact $\beta_1 > 1 > \beta_2$ (equation 19), it is easy to show that

$$0 < \beta_2\delta_1 < \delta_1 < \delta_2 < \beta_1\delta_2 < 1.$$

Thus five intervals are specified, one of which must contain π. A routine check using equation 22 shows that case 1 corresponds to the interval $(0, \beta_2\delta_1)$, 4 with $(\beta_2\delta_1, \delta_1)$, etc. Theorem 18 allows some determination of the values of $\lim_{n\to\infty} E(v_n)$ and $\lim_{n\to\infty} E(1/v_n)$. The former is clearly 0 for case 1 and ∞ for cases 8 and 9. It can only be 0 or finite for cases 4 and 5, since $A(1) < 1$. Similarly, the latter is ∞ for cases 1 and 4, 0 or finite for cases 5 and 8, and 0 for case 9. By theorem 16, neither can be 0 in case 5, since that implies that the other is ∞. Theorems 16 and 17 can be used to determine the value of $\lim_{n\to\infty} E(P_n)$ for three of the five cases. These results, along with those for the other three conditions, are summarized in Table 6.

The incompleteness of our results is all too apparent; we are able to specify $\lim_{n\to\infty} E(P_n)$ only in two out of the five cases for each of the last three conditions and in three out of five in the first. It should be noted that the possibility of employing theorem 17, which yields a formula for $\lim_{n\to\infty} E(P_n)$ under some circumstances, is confined to the middle case of conditions I and II; however, from what is now known of parameter values that apply to data, these appear to be the ones most likely to occur.

TABLE 6. Summary of Asymptotic Results for a Special Case
(See text for explanation)

Condition	$A(1), B(1)$	$A(-1), B(-1)$	Interval Containing π	$\lim\limits_{n\to\infty} E(v_n)$	$\lim\limits_{n\to\infty} E(1/v_n)$	$\lim\limits_{n\to\infty} E(P_n)$
I $\beta_1+\beta_2<2$	$A(1)<B(1)<1$	$A(-1)>B(-1)>1$	$0, \beta_2\delta_1$	0	∞	0
	$A(1)<1<B(1)$	$A(-1)>B(-1)>1$	$\beta_2\delta_1, \delta_1$	0 or finite	∞	—
$\dfrac{1}{\beta_1}+\dfrac{1}{\beta_2}>2$	$A(1)<1<B(1)$	$A(-1)>1>B(-1)$	δ_1, δ_2	finite	finite	P^*
	$1<A(1)<B(1)$	$A(-1)>1>B(-1)$	$\delta_2, \beta_1\delta_2$	∞	0 or finite	—
$\sigma>1$	$1<A(1)<B(1)$	$1>A(-1)>B(-1)$	$\beta_1\delta_2, 1$	∞	0	1
II $\beta_1+\beta_2>2$	$1>A(1)>B(1)$	$1<A(-1)<B(-1)$	$0, \delta_2$	0	∞	0
	$A(1)>1>B(1)$	$1<A(-1)<B(-1)$	$\delta_2, \beta_1\delta_2$	—	∞	—
$\dfrac{1}{\beta_1}+\dfrac{1}{\beta_2}<2$	$A(1)>1>B(1)$	$A(-1)<1<B(-1)$	$\beta_1\delta_2, \beta_2\delta_1$	—	—	—
	$A(1)>B(1)>1$	$A(-1)<1<B(-1)$	$\beta_2\delta_1, \delta_1$	∞	—	—
$\sigma<1$	$A(1)>B(1)>1$	$A(-1)<B(-1)<1$	$\delta_1, 1$	∞	0	1
III $\beta_1+\beta_2>2$	$A(1)<B(1)<1$	$A(-1)>B(-1)>1$	$0, \beta_2\delta_1$	0	∞	0
	$A(1)<1<B(1)$	$A(-1)>B(-1)'>1$	$\beta_2\delta_1, \delta_2$	0 or finite	∞	—
$\dfrac{1}{\beta_1}+\dfrac{1}{\beta_2}>2$	$1<A(1)<B(1)$	$A(-1)>B(-1)>1$	δ_2, δ_1	∞	∞	—
	$1<A(1)<B(1)$	$A(-1)>1>B(-1)$	$\delta_1, \beta_1\delta_2$	∞	0 or finite	—
$\sigma>1$	$1<A(1)<B(1)$	$1>A(-1)>B(-1)$	$\beta_1\delta_2, 1$	∞	0	1
IV $\beta_1+\beta_2>2$	$1>A(1)>B(1)$	$1<A(-1)<B(-1)$	$0, \delta_2$	0	∞	0
	$A(1)>1>B(1)$	$1<A(-1)<B(-1)$	$\delta_2, \beta_2\delta_1$	—	∞	—
$\dfrac{1}{\beta_1}+\dfrac{1}{\beta_2}>2$	$A(1)>B(1)>1$	$1<A(-1)<B(-1)$	$\beta_2\delta_1, \beta_1\delta_2$	∞	∞	—
	$A(1)>B(1)>1$	$A(-1)<1<B(-1)$	$\beta_1\delta_2, \delta_1$	∞	—	—
$\sigma<1$	$A(1)>B(1)>1$	$A(-1)<B(-1)<1$	$\delta_1, 1$	∞	0	1

It should be observed that for conditions I and II equation 20 and theorem 19 imply that the bounds $1/(\sigma+1)$ and $\sigma/(\sigma+1)$, which arise from the requirement that $0 \leq P^* \leq 1$, lie in the second and fourth intervals. For condition I, this suggests the *conjecture* that

$$\lim_{n\to\infty} E(P_n) = \begin{Bmatrix} 1 \\ P^* \\ 0 \end{Bmatrix} \quad \text{if} \quad \begin{Bmatrix} \sigma/(\sigma+1) \leq \pi \leq 1 \\ 1/(\sigma+1) < \pi < \sigma/(\sigma+1) \\ 0 \leq \pi \leq 1/(\sigma+1) \end{Bmatrix}.$$

If this is true, then the asymptotic mean "overshoots" $\pi \geq \frac{1}{2}$, for if

$$P^* = \frac{\pi(\sigma+1)-1}{\sigma-1} \leq \pi$$ then either $\pi \leq \frac{1}{2}$ or $\sigma < 1$. The former is

contrary to choice and the latter violates one of the properties of condition I. How much P^* overshoots π depends upon the value of σ because, as

$\sigma \to \infty$, $P^* \to \pi$, and as $\sigma \to 1$, $P^* = 1$ for $\pi \geqq \sigma/(\sigma + 1) \to \frac{1}{2}$. That is to say, when reward and nonreward are nearly balanced an organism will respond sensitively to small deviations of π from $\frac{1}{2}$; whereas, when nonreward is much more important it will tend more toward probability matching, with some overshooting. For example, if $\pi = 0.75$ and $\sigma = 9$, then $P^* = 0.81$.

For condition II, one might be tempted to conjecture the parallel statement:

$$\lim_{n \to \infty} E(P_n) = \begin{Bmatrix} 1 \\ P^* \\ 0 \end{Bmatrix} \quad \text{if} \quad \begin{Bmatrix} 1/(\sigma + 1) \leqq \pi \leqq 1 \\ \sigma/(\sigma + 1) < \pi < 1/(\sigma + 1) \\ 0 \leqq \pi \leqq \sigma/(\sigma + 1) \end{Bmatrix};$$

however, certain heuristic arguments cast this conjecture into doubt. For, when $0 < \sigma < 1$, then $P^* < \frac{1}{2}$ whenever $\pi > \frac{1}{2}$ and, indeed, $P^* \to 1 - \pi$ as $\sigma \to 0$. This is clearly counter intuitive: it states that the more effective reward is relative to nonreward the less likely the organism is to choose the more often rewarded side. This suggests that the conjecture is wrong or that no organism has $\sigma < 1$.

Another argument suggesting that the conjecture would be in error stems from equation 16 which reduces to

$$E(\log v_{n+1}/v_n) = (\log \beta_1)(1 - \sigma)[E(P_n) - P^*].$$

Since $\sigma < 1$ and $\beta_1 > 1$, the right-hand expression has the same sign as $E(P_n) - P^*$. Thus, if this term is positive, so is $E(\log v_{n+1}/v_n)$, which suggests, but does not prove, that $E(P_{n+1}) > E(P_n)$. Similarly, if $E(P_n) < P^*$, it appears as if $E(P_{n+1}) < E(P_n)$. If so, the system with $\sigma < 1$ is unstable at P^*, with $E(P_n)$ tending either to 0 or 1, depending upon $E(P_0)$.

chapter 5

SUMMARY AND CONCLUSIONS

A. SUMMARY

Throughout this book a universal set U of possible alternatives (stimuli or responses) was assumed given, having the property that for certain finite subsets (always including the two- and three-element sets) a subject can select the elements he thinks most superior (or inferior) according to some specified criterion. Examples of such pairs of sets and criteria are weights and heaviness, events and likelihood of occurring, phonograph records and preference, etc. For certain finite $T \subset U$, a probability measure P_T over the subsets of T was assumed given, in which $P_T(S)$, $S \subset T$, was interpreted as the probability that a subject's choice lies in S when he is forced to make his selection from T according to the (relevant) criterion. For a two-element set $\{x, y\}$, we wrote $P(x, y)$ for $P_{\{x,y\}}(x)$.

The following relation was assumed to hold among these measures:

Axiom 1. *Let T be a finite subset of U such that, for every $S \subset T$, P_S is defined.*

(i) *If $P(x, y) \neq 0, 1$ for all $x, y \in T$, then for $R \subset S \subset T$,*

$$P_T(R) = P_S(R)P_T(S).$$

(ii) *If $P(x, y) = 0$ for some $x, y \in T$, then for every $S \subset T$,*

$$P_T(S) = P_{T-\{x\}}(S - \{x\}).$$

126

This axiom can be viewed as a probabilistic version of both transitivity and independence from irrelevant alternatives, which are familiar from decision theory. Our attention was focused on implications of the axiom and applications of it to several topics in psychology.

By repeatedly applying part ii of the axiom, we can always reduce a problem to pairwise choices or to a set where part i applies. The first important implication (theorem 1) of part i was that all the probabilities can be expressed as a simple function of the pairwise probabilities:

$$P_S(x) = \cfrac{1}{1 + \displaystyle\sum_{y \in S - \{x\}} \cfrac{P(y, x)}{P(x, y)}}.$$

Thus axiom 1 is a possible justification for the almost exclusive attention that has been paid to paired comparisons in the study of choices. Further a relation among triples of pairwise probabilities was established (theorem 2):

$$P(x, z) = \frac{P(x, y)P(y, z)}{P(x, y)P(y, z) + P(z, y)P(y, x)}.$$

This condition is similar to, but distinct from, the one implied by case V of Thurstone's law of comparative judgment. A third general consequence (theorem 3) was the existence of a ratio scale v over any set T for which part i holds and which has the property that for $S \subset T$

$$P_S(x) = \frac{v(x)}{\displaystyle\sum_{y \in S} v(y)}.$$

Although, initially, it appeared as if this result merely implied a collection of extremely local scales, it was shown that they can be amalgamated into a single ratio scale over all of U, provided that axiom 1 holds for sets of three elements, that U is finitely connected (definition 1), and that strong stochastic transitivity (definition 2) is satisfied. It appears from the proof of this result that some sort of multidimensional model satisfying axiom 1 should be possible provided the strong stochastic transitivity condition is dropped. Statistical questions involved in testing axiom 1 were discussed, and references were given to the rather well-developed statistical properties of the v-scale for paired-comparisons data.

It was next shown that if we demand that any theory be independent of the arbitrary unit chosen for the v-scale and if any positive number is a possible scale value, then transformations of v-values must reduce to multiplications by positive constants. This important restriction was applied to the analysis of the so-called time- and space-order errors, showing that we can decompose the data into a matrix that involves only stimulus effects times one that involves only response, or category, effects.

In the final section of Chapter 1 relations between the probabilistic and algebraic theories of choice were explored. It was shown that by defining jnds as in psychophysics we are led to an algebraic system known as a semiorder. Alternatively, by defining a binary relation known as the trace, a weak order results.

Within the psychophysical domain log v was shown to be a Fechnerian scale, in terms of which the pairwise discrimination function is the logistic curve. Assuming that discrimination data satisfy Weber's law (or its linear generalization), the v-scale was shown to be a power function, which, on the basis of magnitude estimation and related experiments, Stevens has urged as "the" psychophysical law for prothetic continua. A sizeable discrepancy was noted between the exponents found by the direct methods and those predicted from discrimination data by the present theory. However, a possible explanation was offered that is based upon an argument designed to explain why there are at least the two types of continua pointed out by Stevens. It was shown that by considering more than one continuum and by making a plausible assumption about the resulting v-scales we are led to at least two, and probably more, classes of continua. Several experimental studies were suggested that should shed some light upon the accuracy of these suggestions.

Next, we explored some relations between axiom 1 and Thurstone's discriminal-process model. Although logically incompatible, case V of the law of comparative judgment is for all practical purposes the same as the pairwise model implied by axiom 1. When the discriminal process idea is extended to sets of three alternatives, it was shown (theorem 7) that no arbitrary uncorrelated discriminal dispersions exist that are consistent with axiom 1. It is not known how large the discrepancy is or whether the models become consistent if correlated dispersions are allowed.

The problem of detecting a signal in the presence of a masking noise, and the influence of the payoffs on the probability of the two types of errors, has been treated in the literature as an application of the Thurstonian model and statistical decision theory. Subjects have been assumed to choose cutoffs on the Thurstonian scale and to respond differently according to whether their observations are above or below the cutoff. We considered replacing the Thurstonian model by an axiom 1 model, subject to the independence-of-unit condition, and we found that (1) the mathematics became simpler, (2) there was little practical difference in the prediction, and (3) there was a major conceptual change.

The cutoff, a notion difficult to generalize beyond one dimension, was replaced by a response bias, which is very easily generalized.

Two questions about rank orderings of alternatives were treated. First, it was shown (theorem 8) that in a plausible ranking model, similar in spirit to axiom 1, the probability of a particular ranking occurring differs, depending upon whether the subject proceeds from the highest element down or the lowest up. Second, it was shown (theorem 9) that the proposed model permits us to estimate pairwise probabilities from ranking data in the obvious way. To show that this result is significant, an example of another possible ranking model was presented in which the same estimating procedure leads to serious errors.

Under the label of utility theory, we examined choices among alternatives—gambles—having the property that the actual payoffs to the subject are contingent upon the outcomes of chance events. A decomposable preference structure (definition 5) is a set of gambles for which the pairwise preference discriminations are statistically independent of the pairwise likelihood discriminations between events, and, for sets of three alternatives, axiom 1 is satisfied by both families of discrimination probabilities. It was shown (theorem 10) that for such a structure either preference discrimination between pairs of pure outcomes is perfect or the space of events is partitioned into, at most, three classes, according to their subjective likelihood of occurring. Three more axioms, similar to some common in utility theory, were shown (theorem 12) to be sufficient to ensure exactly three classes.

The final utility result is of considerable interest because of the sharp test it permits of the theory. Consider the simple game

$$
\begin{array}{cc}
 & \text{I} \quad\ \text{II} \\
\rho & \begin{bmatrix} a & c \\ b & d \end{bmatrix} \\
\bar{\rho} &
\end{array}
$$

where, let us suppose, the entries are sums of money ordered $a > c > d > b$. The subject is required to select a column, the chance event ρ then selects a row, and the subject receives the corresponding payoff. It was shown (theorem 13) that if his choices are described by a decomposable preference structure then his probability of choice, plotted as a function of ρ, must be a step function. This should be contrasted with the ogival function suggested by experience in psychophysics and other areas.

In the final application chapter we took up questions of learning. The general framework of the stochastic learning models was accepted; however, rather than postulate operators that transform a distribution of response probabilities on one trial into their distribution on the next trial, we assumed that axiom 1 holds at each trial and that the operators transform the v-scale on one trial into the v-scale on the next. It was proposed that the scale values be identified with the idea of "response strengths." Two basic, and rather compelling, axioms were imposed upon the operators: they should not depend upon the unknown unit of the v-scale (independence of unit) and they should always result in a legitimate v-scale (positiveness). Since these conditions are not sufficient to determine the mathematical form of the operators, additional assumptions were needed. Three sets leading to three different classes of operators were examined. The first, and the least easy to defend, resulted in the operators that have already been extensively studied, namely, those linear in the probabilities (the alpha model). The second and third sets had an assumption in common: the vector operator was assumed to be a vector of scalar operators (independence from irrelevant alternatives). The distinction between the two models rested fundamentally on whether v is assumed to be unbounded (the beta model) or bounded (the gamma model). An operator of the former type simply multiplies v by a positive constant; one of the latter type effects a linear transformation on v, where the two constants of the transformation are bounded in such a way that the transformed v lies within its bounds. In terms of probabilities, both operators are nonlinear; however, the first is commutative and satisfies the independence-of-path condition, whereas neither is true for the second. An analysis (by R. R. Bush) of rat data in terms of the two-commuting-operator alpha and the beta models was reported. A significant difference in the interpretation of the parameters suggested that experiments can be found for which these two models make differential predictions.

In an attempt to choose among the three learning models we examined what each would predict in a partial reinforcement experiment. Since such an experiment is nothing more than a series of repetitions of the gambling situation discussed in Chapter 3, we assumed that the axioms of a decomposable preference structure, plus the symmetry axiom, would hold on each trial. This led to one of two alternatives: either (1) learning in the experiment produces changes in the likelihood discriminations among events not in the experiment but not perfectly discriminated from the one in the experiment (this can be interpreted as a form of stimulus generalization), or (2) the product of the v-scale values for the two-choice alternatives is a constant from trial to trial. Assuming that the latter held and substituting each of the learning models, we found that the alpha and gamma models both require that there be only a small number of choice probabilities (at most four in the former and two in the latter);

whereas, the beta model was restricted only to the simple beta model. These results seemed to favor the beta model.

In the final section the asymptotic behavior of the beta model for the four-event, subject-experimenter-controlled experiment was considered. Although the results are incomplete, evidence was obtained that the behavior of $\lim_{n\to\infty} E(P_n)$ depends upon the behavior of $\lim_{n\to\infty} E(v_n)$ and $\lim_{n\to\infty} E(1/v_n)$. If either of the latter is 0, then $\lim_{n\to\infty} E(P_n) = 0$ or 1; if both are finite, then an explicit formula for $\lim_{n\to\infty} E(P_n)$ was given. Certain sufficient conditions for $\lim_{n\to\infty} E(v_n)$ and $\lim_{n\to\infty} E(1/v_n)$ to equal 0 and ∞ were given. Nonetheless, some of the more important asymptotic properties of the model are still unknown.

B. CONCLUSIONS

In the preceding chapters an attempt has been made to demonstrate that axiom 1 may serve as an integrating postulate in the study of choice behavior. The axiom was shown to be closely related to traditional, rather well-confirmed ideas, and, at the same time, it led to new results of some empirical interest. Nonetheless, the extent to which it can be considered "true," in the sense that its observable consequences are observed, remains to be seen. It would be nice simply to sit back now and await the experimental returns, but because of the problem mentioned in section 1.A.3—what is an alternative?—all the experimental results are bound to be more or less ambiguous. Until a theory is created that describes how organisms form categories out of the raw material of sensation and teaches us how to detect such categories and the changes in them that result from experience, we can hardly feel secure that the empirical identifications we make of alternatives in this or any other choice theory are appropriate. At present, we must count upon shrewd experimental design and charmed insights as our only hope that the data recorded are about the relevant units of behavior.

It could well happen that axiom 1 will be found to hold when a situation is analyzed one way, but not when viewed another way. Two transparently simple examples may be cited in which a naive interpretation of the axiom would force us to reject it. The first is relevant to both parts of the axiom. Let us suppose that a subject must choose between x and y, there being outcomes O_x^1 and O_y^1, respectively, if the universe is in state S_1, and outcomes O_x^2 and O_y^2 if it is in state S_2. The subject is assumed not to know for certain which state obtains. Now, suppose that a third alternative z is added with outcome O_z independent of the

state; however, let us suppose that the very existence of the third alternative affords some information about which state, S_1 or S_2, holds.   In
such a situation the third alternative is by no means irrelevant to the
choice between x and y, since it indicates to some degree what the outcome will be, and so axiom 1 would not be expected to hold.   Put
another way, if the third alternative is also a discriminative stimulus for
the state of the universe, then, by definition, it will not be irrelevant to
the choice between the first two alternatives whose outcomes depend
upon which state obtains.   .

Our second example is of a different nature and it pertains only to
part i of axiom 1.   Consider a choice from a relatively large set T, e.g.,
a choice among the restaurants in New York City.   It is only sensible to
partition T into a "natural" collection of nonoverlapping subsets, T_1, T_2,
$\cdots$, T_t, e.g., by nationality: French, Chinese, Italian, etc., and first
to choose among these sets.   Let us suppose that none of the pairwise
probabilities is 0 or 1 when choosing among national types, and let
$P_\tau(T_i)$, where $\tau = \{T_1, T_2, \cdots, T_t\}$, denote the probability that the
ith class of restaurants is selected.   Now, with attention confined to that
class, a specific restaurant x is chosen.   Suppose that axiom 1, part i,
is valid in making this choice and that it is done with probability $P_{T_i}(x)$.
Thus the over-all choice probability is given by

$$P_T(x) = P_{T_i}(x)P_\tau(T_i).$$

The question is, does axiom 1 hold for this over-all choice of a restaurant
from T?   Consider some $S \subset T$, e.g., S might be those restaurants in
the theater district.   If $S \subset T_i$, for some i, then the assumption that
axiom 1 holds for the second stage of the process leads to

$$P_{T_i}(x) = P_S(x)P_{T_i}(S),$$

so

$$P_S(x) = P_{Ti}(x)/P_{T_i}(S).$$

From the equation describing the over-all process.

$$P_T(S) = \sum_{y \in S} P_T(y)$$

$$= \sum_{y \in S} P_{Ti}(y)P_\tau(T_i)$$

$$= P_{T_i}(S)P_\tau(T_i).$$

Putting these two statements together we find

$$P_S(x)P_T(S) = \frac{P_{T_i}(x)}{P_{T_i}(S)} P_{T_i}(S)P_\tau(T_i)$$

$$= P_T(x).$$

Thus we conclude that as long as S is contained in one of the subsets of the partition employed at the first stage then axiom 1 will hold if it holds on the second stage of the decision. However, if S cuts across two or more of the subsets of the partition τ, then no such conclusion can be drawn: there simply is not enough information to express $P_S(x)$ in terms of the probabilities of choices at the two stages. It would seem unwise to expect to find axiom 1 holding in such cases.

The problem in practice is to know when a subject decomposes a decision into two or more stages; this is again the problem of knowing how he conceives the alternatives, a difficulty particularly acute in animal experiments. A good deal of data has accumulated to show that something of the order of seven categories is the most that human subjects can cope with in a unitary fashion; see Miller [1956]. If we call a decision that is not subdivided into simpler decisions an elementary choice, then possibly we can hope to find axiom 1 directly confirmed for elementary choices but probably not for more complex ones.

It will be recalled that it was sufficient for most purposes, in particular in extending the ratio scale v over the whole domain, to assume that axiom 1 holds for three-element sets, and it is probably safe to assume that these are always elementary choices when the elements are ends in themselves (not, for example, strategies in the game-theory sense). So the question really is how to interpret a violation of axiom 1 over a set of three alternatives. Do we reject the axiom as false for that domain of stimuli, or do we argue that the alternatives were not what they seemed and that by suitably redefining them the axiom can be saved? If we take the latter alternative, we are led into an extremely subtle problem of scientific methodology and philosophy. If axiom 1 can always be rescued by a redefinition of the alternatives, this suggests that it be accepted as correct and that the alternatives be defined so that it is confirmed. But is this not close to a form of insanity in which truth is by fiat? Why not choose any other relation and set it up as a law, insisting that it is always correct and that other concepts must be changed to make it true? Close though it may be, such an approach is not always insane, provided that certain other conditions are met. Certainly it has been utilized from time to time in physics with great success, and some philosophers have felt themselves forced to the position that certain laws (e.g., conservation of energy) possess empirical content and, at the same time, serve as organizing principles which suggest appropriate definitions in new areas of application.

The question, then, becomes, under what conditions is it not empty to make a statement of the form "for any choice situation there exists a definition of the alternatives such that axiom 1 is true for sets of three alternatives"? I do not know whether philosophers have evolved such a list of conditions in general, but I suspect that the following list will prove to be minimal in this case. First, for a wide variety of situations the axiom will have to be verified for carefully thought out, but independently given, definitions of the alternatives. By and large, these probably will be relatively simple situations. Second, in cases in which the axiom appears to be violated the required redefinition generally will have to result in intuitively acceptable insights into behavior. In many cases one would expect the reaction, "Of course, how did I miss that!" Third, the forced redefinition of the alternatives will have to be comparatively simple. Fourth, the axiom will have to have such rich and useful consequences in all fields of choice behavior when it is coupled with their particular laws that more will be lost by rejecting it than by keeping it. Put another way, it will have to be compatible with, or explain, the laws that have been established in special fields, and together they will have to explain a great deal of observed behavior.

In the preceding chapters I have tried to show that axiom 1's range of application is fairly broad, but it still remains to see just how deep it actually goes. For example, do the suggested modifications of stochastic learning theory actually account for appreciably more learning phenomena than previous theories have? Does the proposed explanation for the several classes of psychophysical scales lead to observed consequences? Do the predicted step functions appear in certain gambling situations? At present, the most one can say is that axiom 1 shows some promising, but inconclusive, symptoms of being a general law of choice behavior.

appendix 1

ALTERNATIVE FORMS OF AXIOM 1

Three alternative forms of part i of axiom 1 are presented. As stated in section 1.C.1, that axiom reads

$$\text{if } R \subset S \subset T, \text{ then } P_T(R) = P_S(R)P_T(S)$$

Let us define $Q_T(S) = 1 - P_T(S)$. Consider the following conditions:

A. *For $R, S \subset T$ such that $R \cap S = \phi$, then $P_T(R) = P_{T-S}(R)Q_T(S)$.*
B. *For $R, S \subset T$ such that $R \cap S = \phi$, then $Q_T(R \cup S) = Q_{T-S}(R)Q_T(S)$.*
C. *For $x, y \in T$, $x \neq y$, then $P_T(x) = P_{T-\{y\}}(x)Q_T(y)$.*

Theorem 20. *Conditions A, B, C, and axiom 1.i are all equivalent.*

PROOF. Axiom 1.i implies A: Suppose $R, S \subset T$ and that $R \cap S = \phi$, then $R \subset T - S \subset T$; so

$$P_T(R) = P_{T-S}(R)P_T(T-S) \qquad \text{(axiom 1.i)}$$

$$= P_{T-S}(R)[1 - P_T(S)] \qquad \text{(probability axioms)}$$

$$= P_{T-S}(R)Q_T(S). \qquad \text{(definition of } Q\text{)}$$

A implies B: Suppose $R, S \subset T$ and that $R \cap S = \phi$, then

$$Q_T(R \cup S) = 1 - P_T(R \cup S) \qquad \text{(definition of } Q\text{)}$$

$$= 1 - P_T(R) - P_T(S) \qquad \text{(probability axioms)}$$

$$= Q_T(S) - P_{T-S}(R)Q_T(S) \qquad \text{(definition of } Q \text{ and condition A)}$$

$$= Q_{T-S}(R)Q_T(S). \qquad \text{(definition of } Q\text{)}$$

135

B implies C: Suppose $x, y \in T$, $x \neq y$, then

$$
\begin{aligned}
P_T(x) &= P_T(x) + [P_T(y) - P_T(y)] + [1 - 1] \\
&= -[1 - P_T(x, y)] + [1 - P_T(y)] \quad &\text{(probability axioms)} \\
&= -Q_T(x, y) + Q_T(y) \quad &\text{(definition of } Q\text{)} \\
&= -Q_{T-\{y\}}(x)Q_T(y) + Q_T(y) \quad &\text{(condition B)} \\
&= P_{T-\{y\}}(x)Q_T(y). \quad &\text{(definition of } Q\text{)}
\end{aligned}
$$

C implies axiom 1.i: Suppose $R \subset S \subset T$. We may assume $S \neq T$, for when $S = T$ axiom 1.i is trivial. Let $y \in T - S$, then

$$
\begin{aligned}
P_T(R) &= \sum_{x \in R} P_T(x) \quad &\text{(probability axioms)} \\
&= \sum_{x \in R} P_{T-\{y\}}(x)Q_T(y) \quad &\text{(condition C)} \\
&= P_{T-\{y\}}(R)Q_T(y). \quad &\text{(probability axioms)}
\end{aligned}
$$

By successively removing elements not in S, we find inductively that

$$
P_T(R) = P_S(R)Q_T(y)Q_{T-\{y\}}(y_1) \cdots Q_{S \cup \{y_k\}}(y_k).
$$

We now show by induction on $|T - S|$ that

$$
Q_T(y)Q_{T-\{y\}}(y_1) \cdots Q_{S \cup \{y_k\}}(y_k) = P_T(S).
$$

If $T - S = \{y\}$, then by condition C and the probability axioms

$$
\begin{aligned}
P_T(S) &= P_{T-\{y\}}(S)Q_T(y) \\
&= P_S(S)Q_T(y) \\
&= Q_T(y).
\end{aligned}
$$

Suppose the assertion is true when $|T - S| = k$, then for $|T - S| = k + 1$, condition C implies

$$
P_T(S) = P_{T-\{y\}}(S)Q_T(y).
$$

Since $|T - \{y\} - S| = k$, we may substitute the induction hypothesis, which proves the assertion, and, therefore, axiom 1.i holds.

FORM OF LATENCY DISTRIBUTION

Throughout the book it has been sufficient to suppose that axiom 1 holds for finite sets—indeed for most purposes three element sets were sufficient. In this appendix one possible generalization of axiom 1 to a class of infinite sets is presented that seems appropriate for studying latency distributions. It is shown that axiom 1.i is equivalent to the distribution that is usually derived in other ways.

Suppose that $S \subset T$ are both intervals (open, closed, or half open as the case may be) of the positive reals, and let $P_T(S)$ denote the probability that the choice lies in S when it is confined to T. Suppose that $0 \leq \tau \leq t$ and consider the intervals:

$$R = [x \mid \tau \leq x \leq t] = [\tau, t]$$

$$S = [x \mid 0 \leq x < \tau] = [0, \tau)$$

$$T = [x \mid 0 \leq x < \infty] = [0, \infty).$$

By the results in appendix 1, a continuous analogue of part i of axiom 1 can be written as the analogue of condition B:

$$Q_{[0,\infty)}([0, t]) = Q_{[\tau,\infty)}([\tau, t]) Q_{[0,\infty)}([0, \tau)). \tag{1}$$

Let us suppose, with no practical loss of generality, that $Q_{[x,\infty)}([x, t])$ is differentiable in t for every x, $0 \leq x \leq t$. If we take the logarithm of equation 1 and differentiate with respect to t we find:

$$\frac{\partial Q_{[0,\infty)}([0, t])/\partial t}{Q_{[0,\infty)}([0, t])} = \frac{\partial Q_{[\tau,\infty)}([\tau, t])/\partial t}{Q_{[\tau,\infty)}([\tau, t])}. \tag{2}$$

Since equation 2 holds for every τ, $0 \leq \tau \leq t$, it can only be a function of t; call it $-\lambda(t)$. Integrating the right-hand expression yields

$$Q_{[\tau,\infty)}([\tau, t]) = \exp\left[-\int_0^t \lambda(x)\, dx + F(\tau)\right],$$

where F is an arbitrary function. However, if we impose the reasonable initial condition that

$$Q_{[\tau,\infty)}([\tau, \tau]) = 1,$$

it is easy to see that F must be such that

$$Q_{[\tau,\infty)}([\tau, t]) = \exp\left[-\int_\tau^t \lambda(x)\, dx\right].$$

Furthermore, if we assume that the initial point of the two intervals is immaterial, i.e.,

$$Q_{[\tau,\infty)}([\tau, t]) = Q_{[0,\infty)}([0, t - \tau]),$$

then it follows that

$$\exp\left[-\int_\tau^t \lambda(x)\, dx\right] = \exp\left[-\int_0^{t-\tau} \lambda(x)\, dx\right].$$

Taking derivatives with respect to t yields

$$\lambda(t) = \lambda(t - \tau),$$

and so λ is a constant.

In the usual derivation leading to this latency distribution the same simple differential equation (equation 2) for Q is arrived at by assuming that if a decision has not been reached by time t then the probability that it is reached in the interval from t to $t + \Delta t$, where Δt is small, can be written $\lambda(t)\, \Delta t$. I consider that approach particularly misleading because it almost appears as if no assumption is being made; however, it is trivial to see that the resulting distribution actually implies equation 1 (axiom 1.i), since

$$\exp\left[-\int_\tau^t \lambda(x)\, dx\right] \exp\left[-\int_0^\tau \lambda(x)\, dx\right]$$
$$= \exp\left[-\int_\tau^t \lambda(x)\, dx - \int_0^\tau \lambda(x)\, dx\right]$$
$$= \exp\left[-\int_0^t \lambda(x)\, dx\right],$$

and, as we know by now, axiom 1.i is actually very strong.

MAXIMUM LIKELIHOOD EQUATIONS FOR THE TWO-ALTERNATIVE, TWO-OUTCOME BETA LEARNING MODEL

The following development is due to R. R. Bush [1957], and it is reproduced here with his permission.

Suppose that there are two alternatives, 1 and 2, and two outcomes, O_1 and O_2, as in the simple T-maze with partial reinforcement. Define the following random variables:

$$x_n = \begin{cases} 1 & \text{if alternative 1 occurs on trial } n, \\ 0 & \text{if alternative 2 occurs on trial } n; \end{cases}$$

$$y_n = \begin{cases} 1 & \text{if outcome } O_1 \text{ follows alternative 1 on trial } n, \\ 0 & \text{if outcome } O_2 \text{ follows alternative 1 on trial } n; \end{cases}$$

$$z_n = \begin{cases} 1 & \text{if outcome } O_1 \text{ follows alternative 2 on trial } n, \\ 0 & \text{if outcome } O_2 \text{ follows alternative 2 on trial } n. \end{cases}$$

Then let

$$P_n = Pr(x_n = 1),$$

$$\pi_1 = Pr(y_n = 1),$$

$$\pi_2 = Pr(z_n = 1).$$

For the simple beta model, which, as we saw in section 4.D.2, is equivalent to the general beta model when there are two alternatives, we have the transition laws

$$P_{n+1} = \begin{cases} \dfrac{\beta_1 v_n(1)}{\beta_1 v_n(1) + v_n(2)}, & \text{if } x_n = 1, \quad y_n = 1, \\[2ex] \dfrac{\beta_2 v_n(1)}{\beta_2 v_n(1) + v_n(2)}, & \text{if } x_n = 1, \quad y_n = 0, \\[2ex] \dfrac{v_n(1)}{v_n(1) + \beta_1 v_n(2)}, & \text{if } x_n = 0, \quad z_n = 1, \\[2ex] \dfrac{v_n(1)}{v_n(1) + \beta_2 v_n(2)}, & \text{if } x_n = 0, \quad z_n = 0. \end{cases}$$

These can also be written in the form

$$P_{n+1} = \begin{cases} \dfrac{\beta_1 P_n}{\beta_1 P_n + Q_n}, & \text{if } x_n = 1, \quad y_n = 1, \\[2ex] \dfrac{\beta_2 P_n}{\beta_2 P_n + Q_n}, & \text{if } x_n = 1, \quad y_n = 0, \\[2ex] \dfrac{P_n}{P_n + \beta_1 Q_n}, & \text{if } x_n = 0, \quad z_n = 1, \\[2ex] \dfrac{P_n}{P_n + \beta_2 Q_n}, & \text{if } x_n = 0, \quad z_n = 0, \end{cases}$$

where $Q_n = 1 - P_n$.   More compactly,

$$P_{n+1} = \frac{P_n}{P_n + \beta_1^{-x_n y_n + (1-x_n)z_n} \beta_2^{(1-x_n)(1-z_n) - x_n(1-y_n)} Q_n}.$$

As noted in section 4.D.1, the operators commute, and so the preceding recurrence relation is readily solved.   Let

$$R_n = \sum_{m=0}^{n-1} [x_m y_m - (1 - x_m)z_m],$$

$$T_n = \sum_{m=0}^{n-1} [(1 - x_m)(1 - z_m) - x_m(1 - y_m)].$$

The solution is then

$$P_n = \frac{P_0}{P_0 + \beta_1^{-R_n}\beta_2^{T_n}Q_0}.$$

This equation gives P_n in terms of the parameters P_0, β_1, and β_2, but it also depends upon the random variables R_n and T_n. Thus a distribution of P_n results.

Assume that a sample of I organisms have identical values of the parameters β_1, β_2, and $K_0 = (1 - P_0)/P_0$. But, according to the last equation, the value of P_n depends upon the random variables R_n and T_n. Thus we need a subscript $i = 1, 2, \cdots, I$ attached to the random variables and to P_n:

$$P_{n,i} = \frac{1}{1 + \beta_1^{-R_{n,i}}\beta_2^{T_{n,i}}K_0}.$$

The likelihood function is

$$L = \prod_i \prod_n P_{n,i}^{x_{n,i}}(1 - P_{n,i})^{1-x_{n,i}}.$$

Setting partial derivatives of log L with respect to K_0, β_1, and β_2 equal to zero, we obtain the estimation equations

$$\sum_i \sum_n x_{n,i} = \sum_i \sum_n P_{n,i};$$

$$\sum_i \sum_n R_{n,i}x_{n,i} = \sum_i \sum_n R_{n,i}P_{n,i};$$

$$\sum_i \sum_n T_{n,i}x_{n,i} = \sum_i \sum_n T_{n,i}P_{n,i}.$$

The left-hand sides of these equations are functions of data only, but the right-hand sides depend upon functions of data as well as upon the parameters—$P_{n,i}$ depends upon the random variables and the parameters. Thus numerical methods are necessary to solve for the maximum likelihood estimates of the three parameters.

appendix 4

OPEN PROBLEMS

At a number of points in the body of this book problems that are presently unsolved have been mentioned; some of these are conceptual, some empirical, and some mathematical. It seems useful to summarize the most important of them in one place, with appropriate references to the earlier discussion. It is not always easy to keep the conceptual separate from the empirical, and it has not been attempted.

A. CONCEPTUAL AND EMPIRICAL

1. Categorization, or What Is an Alternative? (Sections 1.A.3 and 5.B)

Of all the problems to be mentioned, this is beyond any doubt the most important and difficult. Its solution appears to involve developing an appropriate mathematical language to describe the way in which an organism subdivides his environment into manageable chunks and establishing laws governing the relation of one subdivision to another. Without such a theory, it is often difficult to know how to apply or to test a theory of choice. The result in section 3.B.2, giving a possible categorization of events into three classes, affords a lead about how a theory of categorization might be developed.

2. Direct Tests of Axiom 1 (Section 1.C.4)

Extensive empirical studies, unfortunately of a rather tedious nature, need to be undertaken to determine something about the conditions under which axiom 1 holds. At present, only the indirect consequences of the axiom, plus one direct test, give us encouragement that it may be true for a wide class of simple choices. Since the axiom refers only to observables, it should be investigated directly over a variety of domains. The time- or space-order errors that are so often present can be treated by the method described in section 1.F.3.

3. Multidimensional Scaling (Section 1.E.3)

The fact that something like strong stochastic transitivity must be imposed along with axiom 1 to get a unique ratio scale when both perfect and imperfect discriminations exist strongly suggests that we should be able to construct a multidimensional scaling theory within the confines of axiom 1. The crucial condition that leads to multidimensionality seems to be the existence of at least three alternatives, x, y, and z, such that

$$\tfrac{1}{2} \leqq P(x, z) < 1, \qquad \tfrac{1}{2} \leqq P(y, z) < 1, \quad \text{and} \quad P(x, y) = 1.$$

4. Power Law Exponent (Sections 2.B.2 and 2.C.5)

The discrepancy between estimates of the exponent of the power law for prothetic continua based on magnitude estimation data and on discrimination data needs to be adequately explained. A possible, but speculative, explanation was suggested in section 2.C.5; however, the resulting empirical consequences have not yet been checked.

5. Decomposition Axiom (Section 3.B.1)

The decomposition axiom 2 played as important a role in obtaining the interesting results in Chapter 3 as did axiom 1, and since it too concerns observables it should be subjected to direct empirical tests. (Note, however, that this may be deemed unnecessary if positive results are obtained in problem 6.)

6. Gambling Experiment (Section 3.D)

The surprising implication of axioms 1 and 2 that, as α is varied, $P(a\alpha b, c\alpha d)$ must form a step function, provided $P(a, b) = P(c, d) = 1$, should be subjected to test. If the phenomenon is found, it will afford strong indirect support for both axioms 1 and 2 and may render problem 5 superfluous; if not, direct studies of each axiom separately are needed.

7. Experiments to Discriminate Among the Alpha, Beta, and Gamma Learning Models (Chapter 4)

The three learning models described undoubtedly imply noticeably different behavior in certain experimental contexts. If sufficiently radical differences can be found so that data can unambiguously select among the models, then crucial experiments can be designed and run. These tests will have to await either numerical exploration of the beta and gamma models on a computer or successful completion of problem B.4.

8. Implications of Utility Assumptions in Learning Context (Section 4.F)

The assumption that the utility axioms of Chapter 3 hold at each trial of a learning experiment implies two possibilities, one of which is a particular type of stimulus generalization. An experiment to check this prediction in detail is needed, but it does not appear to be easy to design. Assuming that this prediction is rejected, the alternative possibility, coupled with the alpha and gamma learning models, leads to the prediction that there are, at most, four different probabilities of choice. This bears investigation.

B. MATHEMATICAL

1. Interaction of Continua (Sections 2.C.2 and 3)

When Weber's law is not assumed, the explanation suggested for the existence of several classes of psychophysical scales leads to a functional equation that has not been solved. The most important unsolved case is when both continua satisfy the linear generalization of Weber's law. Extend this analysis to n continua.

2. Discriminal Processes (Sections 2.D.2 and 3)

It was shown that axiom 1 implies that the pairwise discrimination function is the logistic curve, and so its derivative yields the discriminal dispersions for differences. Find what discriminal dispersions (correlated or not) for single stimuli, if any, lead to this difference function, or show that none exists. Determine whether correlated dispersions can be found that are compatible with axiom 1 when the discriminal process idea is extended to sets of three alternatives.

3. Decomposable Preference Structures (Chapter 3)

Derive further mathematical properties of decomposable preference structures and determine if there is some version of the expected utility hypothesis that is approximately true.

4. Stochastic Properties of the Beta and Gamma Learning Models (Sections 4.D and E)

At present no nonasymptotic theorems are known for the stochastic processes characterized by the beta and gamma learning operators.

Derive some results; special interest attaches to those that can be used to estimate parameters and to those that establish sharp, observable differences from the alpha model.

5. Asymptotic Properties of the Beta and Gamma Learning Models
(Section 4.G)

Complete the analysis of the asymptotic properties of the beta model and carry out a similar analysis for the gamma model.

BIBLIOGRAPHY

Abelson, R. M., and R. A. Bradley, "A 2 X 2 factorial with paired comparisons," *Biometrics*, **10**, 487–502, 1954.

Adams, E., and S. Messick, "An axiomatization of Thurstone's successive intervals and paired comparisons scaling models," Applied Mathematics and Statistics Laboratory, *Technical Report 12*, Stanford University, 1957.

Arrow, K. J., *Social Choice and Individual Values*, John Wiley and Sons, New York, 1951.

Block, H. D., and J. Marschak, "Random orderings," *Cowles Foundation Discussion Paper No. 42*, Yale University, 1957 (mimeographed).

Bradley, R. A., "Rank analysis of incomplete block designs. III. Some large-sample results on estimation and power for a method of paired comparisons," *Biometrika*, **42**, 450–470, 1955.

———, "Rank analysis of incomplete block designs. II. Additional tables for the method of paired comparisons," *Biometrika*, **41**, 502–537, 1954. (*a*)

———, "Incomplete block rank analysis: on the appropriateness of the model for a method of paired comparisons," *Biometrics*, **10**, 375–390, 1954. (*b*)

———, and M. E. Terry, "Rank analysis of incomplete block designs. I. The method of paired comparisons," *Biometrika*, **39**, 324–345, 1952.

Bush, R. R., "On the testing of a new learning model," The New York School of Social Work, Columbia University, 1957 (mimeographed).

———, E. H. Galanter, and R. D. Luce. "Empirical tests of the beta model." In R. R. Bush and W. K. Estes (Eds.), *Studies in Mathematical Learning Theory*, Stanford University Press, Stanford, 1959.

Bush, R. R., and F. Mosteller, *Stochastic Models for Learning*, John Wiley and Sons, New York, 1955.

———, "A model for stimulus generalization and discrimination," *Psychol. Rev.*, **58**, 413–423, 1951.

———, and G. L. Thompson, "A formal structure for multiple-choice situations."

In R. M. Thrall, C. H. Coombs, and R. L. Davis (Eds.), *Decision Processes*, John Wiley and Sons, New York, 1954, 99–126.

Chipman, J. S., "Stochastic choice and subjective probability," University of Minnesota, 1957 (mimeographed).

Clarke, F. R., "Constant-ratio rule for confusion matrices in speech communication," *J. Acoust. Soc. Am.*, **29**, 715–720, 1957.

Coombs, C. H., "On the use of inconsistency of preferences in psychological measurement," *J. Exp. Psychol.*, **55**, 1–7, 1958.

Cramér, H., *Mathematical Methods of Statistics*, Princeton University Press, Princeton, 1946.

Császár, A., "Sur la structure des espaces de probabilité conditionnelle," *Acta Mathematica*, **6**, 337–361, 1955.

Davidson, D., and J. Marschak, "Experimental tests of a stochastic decision theory," Applied Mathematics and Statistics Laboratory, *Technical Report 17*, Stanford, 1958.

Davidson, D., P. Suppes, and S. Siegel, *Decision Making*, Stanford University Press, Stanford, 1957.

Estes, W. K., "Toward a statistical theory of learning," *Psychol. Rev.*, **57**, 94–107, 1950.

Fano, R. M., "The transmission of information," Research Laboratory of Electronics, *Technical Report 65*, M. I. T., 1949.

Ford, L. R., Jr., "Solution of a ranking problem from binary comparisons," *Amer. Math. Mon.*, Herbert Ellsworth Slaught Memorial Papers, 28–33, 1957.

Galanter, E. H., and R. R. Bush, "Learning and relearning in a T-maze." In R. R. Bush and W. K. Estes (Eds.), *Studies in Mathematical Learning Theory*, Stanford University Press, Stanford, 1959.

Georgescu-Roegen, N., "Threshold in choice and the theory of demand," *Econometrica*, **26**, 157–168, 1958.

———, "The pure theory of consumer's behavior," *Quart. J. Econ.*, **50**, 545–593, 1936.

Guilford, J. P., *Psychometric Methods* (2nd ed.), McGraw-Hill Book Co., New York, 1954.

Gulliksen, H., "A generalization of Thurstone's learning function," *Psychometrika*, **18**, 297–307, 1953.

Hardy, G. H., *A Course of Pure Mathematics*, The Macmillan Company, New York, 1946.

Householder, A. S., and Gale Young, "Weber laws, the Weber law, and psychophysical analysis," *Psychometrika*, **5**, 183–193, 1940.

Hull, C. L., *A Behavior System*, Yale University Press, New Haven, 1952.

———, J. M. Felisinger, A. I. Gladstone, and H. G. Yamaguchi, "A proposed quantification of habit strength," *Psychol. Rev.*, **54**, 237–254, 1947.

Irwin, F. W., "An analysis of the concepts of *discrimination* and *preference*," *Amer. J. Psychol.*, **71**, 152–165, 1958.

Licklider, J. C. R., "Basic correlates of the auditory stimulus." In S. S. Stevens (Ed.), *Handbook of Experimental Psychology*, John Wiley and Sons, New York, 1951, 985–1039.

Luce, R. D., "On the possible psychophysical laws," *Psychol. Rev.*, **66**, 81–95, 1959.

———, "A probabilistic theory of utility," *Econometrica*, **26**, 193–224, 1958.

———, "Semiorders and a theory of utility discrimination," *Econometrica*, **24**, 178–191, 1956.

———, and W. Edwards, "The derivation of subjective scales from just noticeable differences," *Psychol. Rev.*, **65**, 222–237, 1958.

Luce, R. D., and H. Raiffa, *Games and Decisions*, John Wiley and Sons, New York, 1957.

Marschak, J., "Norms and habits of decision making under uncertainty," *Mathematical Models of Human Behavior*, Dunlap and Associates, Stamford, 1955, 45–54.

Miller, G. A., "The magical number seven, plus or minus two: some limits on our capacity for processing information," *Psychol. Rev.*, **63**, 81–97, 1956.

———, "Sensitivity to changes in the intensity of white noise and its relation to masking and loudness," *J. Acoust. Soc. Am.*, **19**, 609–619, 1947.

Miller, N. E., "Experimental studies of conflict." In J. McV. Hunt (Ed.), *Personality and the Behavior Disorders*, Ronald Press, New York, 1944, 431–465.

Mosteller, F., and P. Nogee, "An experimental measurement of utility," *J. Pol. Econ.*, **59**, 371–404, 1951.

Ramsey, F. P., *The Foundations of Mathematics*, Harcourt, Brace and Co., New York, 1931.

Rényi, A., "On a new axiomatic theory of probability," *Acta Mathematica*, **6**, 285–335, 1955.

Savage, L. J., *The Foundations of Statistics*, John Wiley and Sons, New York, 1954.

Shannon, C. E., and W. Weaver, *The Mathematical Theory of Communication*, University of Illinois Press, Urbana, 1949.

Shepard, R. N., "Stimulus and response generation: a stochastic model relating to distance in psychological space," *Psychometrika*, **22**, 325–345, 1957.

———, "Stimulus and response generation: tests of a model relating generalization to distance in psychological space, *J. Exp. Psychol.*, **55**, 509–523, 1958.

Spence, K. W., *Behavior Theory and Conditioning*, Yale University Press, New Haven, 1956.

Stevens, S. S., "On the psychophysical law," *Psychol. Rev.*, **64**, 153–181, 1957.

———, "Mathematics, measurement, and psychophysics." In S. S. Stevens (Ed.), *Handbook of Experimental Psychology*, John Wiley and Sons, New York, 1951, 1–49.

———, and E. H. Galanter, "Ratio scales and category scales for a dozen perceptual continua," *J. Exp. Psychol.*, **54**, 377–411, 1957.

Swets, J. A., and T. G. Birdsall, "The human use of information. III. Decision making in signal-detection and recognition situations involving multiple alternatives," *Transactions of the I.R.E., Professional Group on Information Theory*, IT-2, 1956.

Tanner, W. P., Jr., and R. Z. Norman, "The human use of information. II. Signal detection for the case of an unknown signal parameter," *Transactions of the I.R.E., Professional Group on Information Theory*, PGIT-4, 1954.

Tanner, W. P., Jr., and J. A. Swets, "A decision-making theory of visual detection," *Psychol. Rev.*, **61**, 401–409, 1954. (*a*)

———"The human use of information. I. Signal detection for the case of the signal known exactly," *Transactions of the I.R.E., Professional Group on Information Theory*, PGIT-4, 1954. (*b*)

Thurstone, L. L., "The learning function," *J. Gen. Psychol.*, **3**, 469–493, 1930.

———, "Psychophysical analysis," *Amer. J. Psychol.*, **38**, 368–389, 1927. (*a*)

———, "A law of comparative judgment," *Psychol. Rev.*, **34**, 273–286, 1927. (*b*)

von Neumann, J., and O. Morgenstern, *Theory of Games and Economic Behavior* (2nd ed.), Princeton University Press, Princeton, 1947.

Young, T. T., "Studies of food preferences, appetite, and dietary habit. VII. Palatibility in relation to learning and performance," *J. Comp. Physiol. Psychol.*, **40**, 37–72, 1947.

INDEX

151

152   Index

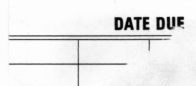

DATE DUE